THE TRAINING OFFICER

DO YOU HAVE WHAT IT TAKES?

David McGlynn

Disclaimer: The recommendations, advice, descriptions, and methods in this book are presented solely for educational purposes. The author and publisher assume no liability whatsoever for any loss or damage that results from the use of any of the materials in this book. Use of the material in this book is solely at the risk of the user.

The views, opinions, and suggestions throughout this book are those of the author, David McGlynn and are not endorsed nor any reflection of the Department of the Army or the Department of Defense Fire & Emergency Services.

Copyright © 2023 by David McGlynn

Published by The Firefighter Book Club
A Division of the Red Helmet Training Group
10601 Church Street #107, Rancho Cucamonga, CA 91730
www.FirefighterBookClub.com
(909)466-4671

ISBN: 978-1-959240-04-4 (Paperback)
ISBN: 978-1-959240-05-1 (Hardback)

Library of Congress Cataloging-in-Publication Data

Library of Congress Control Number 2023952028

David McGlynn – Author

Frank Ricci - Foreword

Contributing Authors – Mike "Champ" Ciampo, P.J. Norwood, Steve Prziborowski, Conor Miller, Jim Moss, Tom Merrill, Mike Scotto, Larry "Uncle" Conley, Scott Little, Steve Hamilton and Frank Viscuso

Cover Photos by Brian Rhodes

Managing Editor – Jesse Quinalty

Copy Edited by Judith Glick-Smith

All rights reserved. No part of this publication may be reproduced, distributed, stored in a retrieval system, or transmitted in any form or by any means, including photocopying, recording, or other electronic or mechanical methods without the author's prior written permission.

Acknowledgements

All my FE people; Ricci, PJ, Hamy, Priz, Champ, Jim Moss, Viscuso, Uncle Larry, Silvernail, Ric Jorge, Pete, Mark, Eileen, and Tommy Brennan, I never had the fortune of meeting him, but absolutely loved his passion for training our beloved fire service, thank you for paving the way.

Chief Rhodes our new Commander, looking forward to supporting your vision and following your lead.

Diane, you have been a huge supporter of me and what I do, I appreciate you more than words can explain, thank you, I love you!

Bobby Halton, this is for you too, you took a chance on me (as you did so many of us) and allowed me to take my message to a bigger stage, your stage. I will never forget that and will always appreciate it. You taught me about the importance of the standard. Rest Easy Chief, we miss you every day!

Jesse, thanks for trusting me enough to do this book, it means more than you know. We are going to do great things together!

The Iselin (NJ) Fire District 9, NAS Brunswick (ME) Fire Department, Raven Rock (PA) Fire Department, Carlisle Barracks (PA) Fire Department, West Point (NY) Fire Department, and Letterkenny (PA) Fire Department.

The DA F&ES Training Network (aka Working Group). Keep making our people better each and every day!

All who have contributed to this project, your work is both meaningful and greatly appreciated. This book would be empty without it.

Scott, for being the meaning of a best friend and defining loyalty. Thank you for encouraging me to start doing this stuff.

The fellas at the West Point Fire Department, for helping me grow into my roles and responsibilities as a training officer. Appreciate all the work we did, and you continue to do, which I am proud to showcase throughout this book.

13 Hose, my team, "my guys," I want the fire service to know who you are and what we are about. We are the standard! Thank you for your dedication.

Dedication

This book is dedicated to you, the reader, the person who is trying to learn more about training others. Without people like you who are constantly striving to learn more so they can bring that knowledge to their organization, the future of our fire service would be doomed. Thank you for being a student of the craft and for taking the time to read this book.

This book is also dedicated to all the great instructors I had at Middlesex County (NJ) Fire Academy, Bucks County (PA) Fire Training, Alabama Fire College, Maryland Fire Rescue Institute, Maine Fire Training and Education, Harrisburg Area (PA) Community College Public Safety, Orange County (NY) Fire Training Center, and Franklin County (PA) Public Safety Training Center. Especially to Instructor Spirko for never giving up on me and coaching me through it. Wouldn't be here today if you didn't, thank you!

To Mr. IlVento and Mrs. Dinicola, thank you both for never giving up on me, and teaching me what it takes to be a good teacher and role model.

My parents, my first mentors and first leaders. You both taught me the importance of service to others before self. Your encouragement, guidance, and teachings cannot be matched, I only hope I can have half as much wisdom as you both did so I can continue my path. To my brothers (Richie & Pete) and my sister (Kelly), thank you for the life lessons and support. Thank you for encouraging me and teaching me how to be strong.

My children, Angela and Michael: You are what makes life tolerable, you both are my top students. I strive to be a better man and a better example every day because of you. My wish is for you to both develop into amazing people who create their own level of success. You both have greatness within you. Never let anyone or anything prevent you from using your natural ability to be great! Being your father is my highest honor; I am blessed for the opportunity to be a part of your development. Be the best version of yourself and you will lead a happy life.

My wife, Krissy, my best friend: You are my rock, my muse, and my support. Without your support and encouragement, I couldn't do what I do. You give me strength when I am weak, you cheer me on when I think I'm out of the game.

I Love You All!

Contents

Acknowledgements iii
Dedication..iv
Foreword..1
Welcome to Training!..5
The Training Officer 9
Training Officers Are Leaders, Too!.......................................27
Challenges for the Training Officer..45
Tunnel Vision and Ego 69
Organizational and Cultural Dynamics 87
Coaching, Mentoring, and Mutual Trust 107
Building a Training Network 121
Training Program Development 141
Quality vs. Quantity... 163
Having What It Takes 183
Suggested Training Requirements.. 199
Bibliography... 203

Foreword

By Frank Ricci

When one walks into the Fire Department of New York's training academy on the Rock you are hit with words etched into the wall, "Let no man's ghost come back to say my training let me down." The words draw on the inherent dangers of the job and the extraordinary responsibility facing training officers.

"Death" and "injury" are printed on a card in every firefighter's hand and there is not a competent firefighter who wouldn't make their spouse a widow and their kids parentless for the community they serve.

Only, this is not blind dedication. We should endeavor to do better and realize that as firefighters we don't rise to meet expectations, we fall to our level of training and functional fitness. It is the position of training officer that makes the difference, effecting outcomes and impacting lives.

Assistant Chief David McGlynn takes us past the perils of failure and inspires us to lead with passion, purpose, persistence, and professionalism. David knows what it takes to be a great training officer and walks us through the critical components of this cornerstone position.

David is a consummate professional who has projected a consistent set of values and standards throughout his career. Insofar his operational and administrative effectiveness is concerned I have found him to be a serious, proficient, and dedicated individual who is quit, non-overbearing and in possession of a warm personality and sense of humor who regularly goes out of his way contributing to the betterment of the fire service.

I have witnessed him perfect his message on the national stage at the Fire Department Instructors Conference (FDIC) and grow into a great instructor whose command presence has earned him the respect of his peers on a national level.

This is an individual who is approachable and wants to hear from you. Chief McGlynn has found a way to passionately advocate for the fire service, "Eight days a week."

He now brings that vision and message to your hands through this groundbreaking manuscript that goes beyond the textbooks to position you for success. David is a humble and thoughtful individual who does not shy away from self-reflection in this book bringing you an honest look into this critical position.

He understands and has demonstrated throughout his career that a successful training officer should view their position not through the lens of rank and power but through mentoring and providing positive influence while building trust.

Do You Have What It Takes?

The training officer is an educator. The word "educator" is derived from the Latin word "educare" which means to "draw out from within or to lead fourth." David seeks through his writing to draw out the very best in you, to make sure you have what it takes!

Chief McGlynn challenges the reader to think through situations with exercises to bridge understanding and provides foundational information that you can build on in each chapter.

He also asks that readers be honest with themselves to ensure the reason for their interest in the position is more than a vehicle for a future promotion, that it is viewed as a calling and, when done right, can be the most important role in your organization.

He takes us past instructional methodologies and stale textbooks that leave us with more questions than answers. David opens a window to witness the ins and outs of the training officer so readers can position themselves for the tasks ahead and strive for excellence.

The book goes beyond theory by providing tangible takeaways on how to build training programs and networking solutions. Simply, he doesn't want you to suck at your job! He wants you to develop your latent talent and provide vision and direction. David doesn't leave you in the darkness but, through his writing, gives you the lessons you need to search for the light.

He recognizes that it is the training officer that can have the largest impact on the organization. And, yes, in this position of responsibility, accountability to the Chief, firefighters, and the citizens can be demanding. It is this same scrutiny that will push you to excel and to be an advocate for proper training.

It is paramount to understand that if you do your job right your impact will allow you to share in small measure when a rescue is made, a firefighter gets themselves out of being jammed up, or a difficult emergency is mitigated safely, efficiently, and in an effective manner. It is the training officer that sets the standard.

Our nation's first Drillmaster Baron de Steuben summed up the difference between European and American troops in one word: "Why." The European teaching model of command-and-follow did not work well with the American militia. The American spirit dictated that the instructor explained the why and how for each lesson. With this information, the individual soldier would better understand the maneuvers, which would create a more effective fighting unit.

You see, it is imperative that we heed this lesson from the past of explaining the "why" and move to the future by following Chief David McGlynn's advice and wisdom to ensure predictable outcomes positioning yourself to succeed in the role of training officer.

Foreword

Whether you need to build a training program, need to justify a budget, or build a training network, this book will set you on the right path.

It was Tom Brennan who taught us, "You can never learn enough about something that can kill you." It is David McGlynn who can teach you how to prepare and succeed in the position of training officer while ensuring the trust placed in you would not lead to any meandering ghost questioning their fate and training.

In Liberty,

Frank Ricci

Author of the Book *Command Presence*
Ret. Battalion Chief & Drillmaster, New Haven, CT
Lead Plaintiff in Landmark SCOTUS Case
FDIC & Fire Engineering Advisory Board

Preface

Welcome to Training!

My decision to write this book did not come easy, but I felt through my own experiences it was much needed. Over the past 22+ years, I have had the opportunity to serve as a municipal firefighter in New Jersey as well as a firefighter for the federal government, where I served as a company officer, training officer, and currently as a Chief Officer. I experienced firsthand the expectations that firefighters, community, and leadership held for a high-quality training program and training officer.

This book aims to train current training officers and aspiring training officers to prepare them for the true roles and responsibilities of a training officer. The book's primary objective is to offer motivation to training officers and ensure passion in their development, which is critical when encouraging other people to be as enthusiastic as they are in their duties.

Why this book?

It is my intent to offer the tools needed for the development of a good training officer while proving that the training officer is the most important person in an organization. I have seen the inefficiencies in training officers. In this contemporary world, it can be argued that all training officers care about is performing the training required by a checklist. Moreover, this method proves to be inefficient and fails to develop the necessary training needed for a well-fortified, progressive, and proficient training program. In addition, my hope is that, at a minimum, the purpose and value of this book is to prevent training officers from taking the position for the wrong reasons and, instead, inspire those who want to build strong teams to become training officers for the right reasons.

Many people claiming to be training officers do it because of the promotion benefits or because of their lazy nature, simply thinking that this new role will get them out of doing the "hard" work. Because firefighting requires technical experience, many people unable to cope with firefighting demands prefer to be training officers because they think this will prevent them from being exposed as a person unable to "hack" it. This ideology creates lazy training officers who transfer that zero ambition towards their team.

The fire service has produced several training officers who are faking their whole career and, therefore, they provide unsatisfactory results for the organization. Innovativeness becomes crucial because it ensures that training officers are more creative in accomplishing their tasks. Training officers who lack the ability or desire to conduct a true assessment of their mission needs end up creating a program made of poor training which begets poor operations.

This book also discusses the many types of challenges a training officer will encounter. Some challenges include budget strain, documentation, recruitment, retention, personalities, annual requirements, and scheduling.

The training officer helps shape and develop the operational skillset needed for the services that are expected to be provided. This book will help prepare up-and-coming training officers while refreshing current ones of why incorporating passion into their program development is important. This book breaks down the much-needed qualities of a good training officer into chapters while covering the different challenges and levels of maturity one passes through while growing into a leader and becoming a training officer. Readers will experience a "gut check" about their own qualities as training officers. We will expose some of the traits of a bad training officer and will offer some suggestions of what qualities a good training officer should have. Sadly, when we put on rank, we either lose our passion for the job and we develop those bad traits or we take on a training officer position with no experiences or credibility to support us being a subject matter expert. This combination results in the inevitable failure of our training program. As training officers, we need to understand why training is so important and design an atmosphere where everyone strives to be better than they were yesterday.

As you continue reading, we will further discuss leadership and how networking and team building abilities are fundamental to a progressive fire department training program. Lastly, we will discuss the process of finding the correct balance in training about event scheduling. Training is a gradual process that requires a series of steps to succeed.

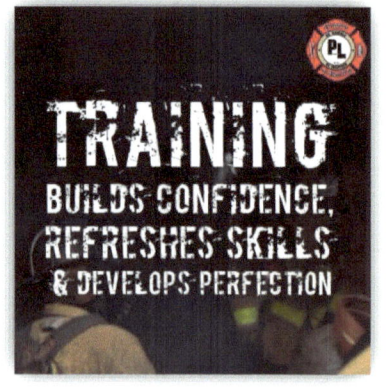

This book is designed to pass on some things that have worked for me in my tenure as a training officer, in hopes that you can use some of it in your educational development as a training officer.

So, let's see if you have what it takes to be a training officer.

Welcome to Training!

A VIEW FROM EXPERIENCE

By: Mike "Champ" Ciampo,
Lieutenant Fire Department of New York (FDNY)

Michael N. Ciampo first joined the fire service in 1979 as a fourth-generation volunteer firefighter. In 1985, his professional career started with the District of Columbia Fire Department (DCFD), and, in 1990, he was hired by the Fire Department of New York (FDNY). He attended John Jay College of Criminal Justice and earned a BA degree in Fire Science. He is a nationally recognized instructor, teaching truck company operations and tower ladder classes to departments around the country. He writes the back page column 'On Fire' for Fire Engineering magazine and is featured in their Truck Company Training Minutes videos.

Be Dynamic, Be Knowledgeable, Be Creative

Right after 9-11 my career took a serious change, being promoted to Lieutenant and having a whole new set of responsibilities. I had suddenly become the boss, leader, administrator, and instructor. Maybe I was lucky because the job took a drastic change and we saw an influx of new firefighters coming onto the job, class after class. Although we were still working on the pile and recovering physically and mentally, the daily runs to fire and emergencies were still there. However, in a few short months these runs had a new cadre of firefighters responding to them. Young, eager, enthusiastic, and aggressive was what we saw in them, but we also saw inexperience.

It's easy to shape firefighters when you're in a busy firehouse because they're out the door numerous times of the day. On the automatic fire alarm runs you can point out a building construction concern, get a floor layout or which stairwell would you stretch out of? On some of these runs as we would drive back to quarters, I'd have the chauffeur pull over at a peculiar building and throw a situation at the firefighters in the crew cab and now they had to perform. Throwing ladders in a below grade courtyard, laddering a sidewalk scaffold and then pulling the ladder up onto the platform to a window out of reach of the tower ladder. Or maybe we were just coming down the stairs, smelling like a burnt pot of food on the stove from the run. We spotted a door with numerous locks on it and angle iron preventing the Halligan tool from getting a good purchase, and we would drill on it. If we did catch a fire, we held a company informal critique so we could all hear what the other firefighters saw and did. It's easy to shape your firefighters as a team, even if one of them ran into issues or had problems, encourage them to learn from this fire, and offer them some suggestions for if and when that situation happens again. Chastising them can create unfaithfulness in their boss and create hardships between you and the team.

Do You Have What It Takes?

Unfortunately, in our field we are seeing more and more firefighters coming onto the job with no mechanical skills or a trade. They haven't been exposed to tools like many of the older firefighters have. Simple, realistic, and basic drills for these firefighters must be performed. It might seem irrelevant for the carpenter in the group to hit 16 penny nails into a 4x4, but for the kid who can't swing a hammer it can be embarrassing. Training officers must look into their staff and size-up what needs to be done to give their firefighters experience with the tools and equipment carried on the apparatus. We once took both of our picnic tables and intertwined them with a victim pinned by a street sign, metal studs, wood studs, rebar, a piece of fencing and PVC piping resembling a collapse. The firefighters had to work in all sorts of positions to cut the material with a few of our cordless cutters. The look on some of their faces when they learned that the reciprocal saw's blade could be inserted in two positions was amazing, but they'd never been exposed to that before. So be creative, use materials to help get the basics down. Scrap plywood and pallets are beneficial for all firefighters to practice using saws.

Have fun when you train; kid with them with a nickname or a little humor but be the first to show them how to do it. Encourage them to try again and again. Doing something once doesn't make anyone an expert. Repetition of an element provides them with the opportunity to do it properly at 0400 hours when the pressure is on to save a life. When you lecture, be upbeat, involve the crowd, ask questions, shake hands, and introduce yourself and have them tell you a quick bit about themselves and their department so you can be on their level. Mix funny slides into your program to get a laugh but keep it real. Show them that things do go bad on our job and at incidents and emphasize that we want to try and eliminate these things through training.

Be ambitious when you train. Train your crew to represent you, your company, and your department. When one firefighter messes up, it puts a stain on all of us. Remember, you can't be an expert in everything because we have so many disciplines; use some of your firefighters, who may be subject matter experts in certain fields (i.e., ropes, shoring, Haz-Mat, and meters) to train the other members of your company. Be the team leader and train each day, each tour, and whenever the opportunity presents itself.

Amateurs train to get it right; Professionals train so they don't get it wrong!

Lt. Michael Ciampo

FDNY

Chapter 1

The Training Officer

So, you want to be a training officer! Do you have what it takes? Well…do you?!?

When I first became a training officer, I was promoted to the position at the most prestigious military installation in the world. Walking around the campus, I felt overwhelmed by its rich history and traditions, accentuated by medieval and gothic architecture. Treading the same grounds where many of America's greatest leaders were educated instilled a sense of awe in me, which was a bit scary.

To further that anxiety, I inherited a training program that had an expectation of high-speed functions and a desire to meet the installation's reputation of being the best. This was not a place where you could "fake it till you make it." I realized soon that to prove worthy of being a member of such history at an establishment enriched in duty and honor, I must make an attempt to be a student of the craft while being responsible for facilitating and managing the program.

Through my tenure there I gained a ton of experience and developed many great memories, one of the memories that sticks with me the most is a statue of General George Patton. General Patton repeated his first year as a cadet, and when asked once "how could you be such a great wartime General, yet you struggled academically?" He answered, "I guess I couldn't find the library."

This story is not found in many history lessons or books, but if you have the opportunity to be a part of the culture there, you will learn the intimacy of the subliminal message behind why Patton's statue is placed how and where it is.

You see, General Patton's statue looks off towards what is known as Trophy Point and behind it a great landscape with the Hudson River. Yet, to his back is the library. While Patton stands proud looking off with his binoculars in his hand, the library stands right behind him. He appears unaware of where it is. I have always admired that story because in truth, I was not the most educated, nor the best at what I did. However, I tried hard, learned as much as I could and gained as many real-life experiences as I could.

"A View from Experience" General George S. Patton Monument, West Point, NY

These real-life experiences have helped prepare me in my journey throughout the fire service enhancing my ability to design and create programs and develop and nurture future firefighters. General Patton proved that, though education is important, what is even more important is the ability to apply skills adeptly in critical moments. That ability comes with experience coupled with training and education. Therefore, I have dubbed Patton's statue as "A View From Experience." This title headlines each contributed section featuring insights from leaders and training officers across the U.S.

The experience part is up to you, don't just read this book. Go out and do what you will be training your student firefighters to do next.

A training officer who lacks efficiency leads to inadequately trained firefighters. This, in turn, results in subpar skill execution, ultimately tarnishing the reputation of the fire department.

This chapter describes the role of the training officer including elements and characteristics. Fire departments offer a multitude of services all of which are crucial activities to society, including public safety. Firefighters in the field should receive the necessary training to ensure that they are proficient in delivering those services when needed. Being that there is such an essential requirement for an efficient training program, someone needs to facilitate, and manage said program. The person responsible for overseeing the organization of a fire department training program is the training officer.

> *"The person responsible for overseeing the organization of a fire department training program is the training officer."*

Throughout this chapter, you should gain an understanding of what it means to be a training officer. A good training officer can improve a department's image by developing firefighters' efficiency. One thing worth mentioning is that training officers should also be efficient in their jobs. Still, without proper dedication by the firefighters in their training, the result will be a failed training program surrounded by limited skills due to the lack of proficiency.

According to this analysis, adequate coordination between the firefighter and the training officer is crucial to ensure that they get the required skills that will benefit them in their firefighter responsibilities. Many people, including the training officers, fail to recognize how vital their duties are in managing the organization. They are the department's core because they represent all the training officer attributes, including coaching, mentoring, executive actions, and company officer duties. Without these core elements the fire department may be subject to failure.

Elements and Characteristics of a T.O.

Empathy

Empathy relates to the ability to understand and share each other's feelings. A training officer should have empathy in order to relate to different firefighters and their individual emotional characteristics. Each individual in an organization has different experiences. Each of those experiences affect how they became who they are in the future. This may result in some of the firefighters not being able to perform at the same speed or level as other firefighters.

While some firefighters may be really good test-takers or fully capable of executing their skills both during training and on emergencies, others may need that one-on-one focus to build their motivation. This may include improving their desire to perform better and understanding what they need to do to improve.

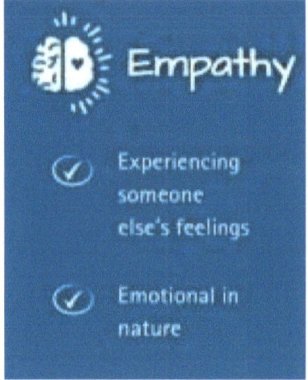

How a training officer treats one firefighter may be different from how they treat another firefighter. In the same manner, if a training officer were to have the same performance expectation of each of their firefighter's abilities and skillsets, they may eliminate or reduce the motivation for some individuals, affecting the overall fire department's efficiency. Because of how crucial this characteristic is, the training officer should have the experience of being a firefighter in their career. This experience ensures that they understand how it feels to be in that situation, preventing poor judgment.

Furthermore, it will ensure firefighters know how they think when they have unbearable tasks. This understanding, otherwise called empathy, will ensure that the training officer knows how to approach and understand each firefighter, thereby boosting their efficiency in training and the field.

Sympathy

Sympathy pertains to having an awareness of and demonstrating a level of compassion for another individual's adversity. Many people confuse sympathy and empathy because of their close relation. Sympathy involves understanding someone else's misfortunes from your perspective, while empathy relates to understanding their situation by putting yourself in their shoes. A sympathetic training officer considers what an individual is going through and ensures better handling of the situation while creating a culture that supports each member to build cohesion.

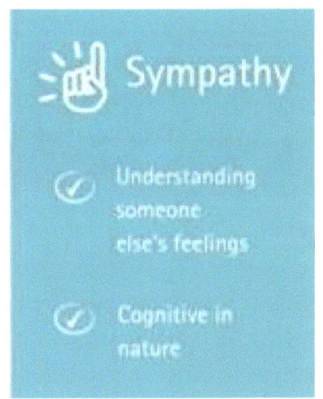

Furthermore, they realize that a firefighter may be dealing with other issues that may be casting a shadow over their performance and they may not be efficient in learning new skills. They may need additional time or other duties assigned to them before they attain full recovery.

Moreover, sympathy allows training officers to understand that not all firefighters have the same learning ability enabling them to be more aware of their personnel and improve their ability to design a training program that is conducive to a positive and developmental environment.

Training Officer Leadership

Leadership is vital for any training officer because it ensures that the firefighters get behind them and perform their training programs effectively. Furthermore, it removes any blind followers. Blind followers are a significant setback because they perform everything like robots and fail to differentiate between what looks right and what is wrong.

Training officers should have good leadership qualities to differentiate between blind and efficient followers. A training officer should take charge and be the focal point to earn respect from those that look upon them. According to this analysis, a training officer should not seek support from the firefighters but should seek their trust. Trust is an element that many people get by showing they can be effective and are credible.

For example, an experienced training officer understands the types of things that can occur in the field; this experience can help them earn the firefighters' trust by teaching these experiences to them. The more the firefighters feel they can rely on their training officer in such incidences, the more they trust them. Trust between the training officer and the firefighters is essential in building an efficient training program. With better trust comes respect, ensuring better workplace relationships.

Good Follower

It is essential to understand that organizations have a different chain of commands. Some organizations have an official position designated to the training officer, while others may have those roles and responsibilities as an extra assigned duty. Nonetheless, those positions typically have a set of tasks allocated to them by the fire chief. Being a good follower requires respect and the willingness to perform duties according to the department's operating procedures.

Training officers cannot be good followers of the rules if they lack experience from their early firefighting days. They should have that experience to understand the importance of respecting the procedures or "rules" above their jurisdiction. If they have the combination of experience and understanding of the rules, they can have tough conversations with their firefighters.

As a training officer you'll also need to have the ability to have tough conversations with your firefighters which include making them aware that they are not performing to the expectations of the organization's needs and the training officer's objectives. They should have the Knowledge, Skills, and Abilities (KSA's) required to be proficient in the demanding tasks expected of firefighters. The training officer's responsibility is to design a training program that offers development in those required KSA's and ensure all firefighters are able to meet those expectations, while balancing the different skillsets of each firefighter. Firefighters occasionally may not perform at a highly functioning level; the training officer needs to be able to adjust their methodology to those individual learner needs.

If a member is not meeting the performance expectations simply due to insubordination or an inability to truly execute the required skills, the training officer also needs to be able to set the standard and hold members accountable to meeting that standard. This activity is what relates to having tough conversations.

Good Coaching

Good coaching relates to making people understand how good they can be if they implement the correct activities in their program. Furthermore, it ensures that individuals know that the answers to their problems exist within themselves. Webster's dictionary defines coaching as *a method of directing, instructing, and* **training** *a person or group of people with the aim of achieving some goal or* **developing** *specific skills*. A better understanding of these concepts ensures that the training officer is aware of and understands their people's full potential. In order for a training officer to be a good coach they should ensure that they realize the full potential of the firefighters. Many firefighters can possess hidden talents which can make them better firefighters.

The training officer should ensure that they realize the full potential of their firefighters to showcase their talents both on the training grounds and in the field. An efficient training officer brings with them better training which supports the preparation and proficiency needed to ensure community safety through safer, more skilled performance by their firefighters.

Coach Ara Parseghian - Notre Dame Football

A good coach understands the difference between coaching and mentoring. This quote by Coach Parseghian literally sums up how to coach your people for today while mentoring them for their future.

> *"a good coach can show his players what they can be."*
>
> Coach Ara Parseghian

Mentoring

Mentoring involves someone with a different or increased level of experience providing knowledge to others to ensure their development. Mentors provide four essential activities, including **guiding, supporting, encouraging,** and **teaching**. These elements are what a good training officer incorporates into their programs and methods to make themselves efficient. A training officer should be a mentor to ensure they get the best from their firefighters. Using the training officer's experience as a firefighter can guide and teach the individuals they are training how to be better firefighters. Because they understand the role from their previous work, their successes and failures can be the basis for their training. They will lead the firefighters on what to do and what not to do, ensuring their success as firefighters. Furthermore, they can teach them what lifestyle to adapt to in an effort to get the best out of their physical abilities.

A mentoring training officer teaches the firefighters the training basics and advises them on lifestyle choices. Lifestyle has a significant impact on a firefighter's performance, and it is an activity that the training officer should incorporate. Firefighting is a unique job because of the high risks involved, and firefighters should have a healthy lifestyle that keeps them active. A better lifestyle allows for better performance which yields productivity. Mentoring includes encouraging and supporting the firefighters.

Essentially being a mentor as a training officer is like molding clay. Your firefighters are the ball of clay, and the intent for the training officer should be to create something magnificent out of that ball of clay… a masterpiece!

A Desire to Develop Others

Training officers should want to develop their firefighters. This is why experience is vital for any training officer. Their expertise in the field allows them to understand the need to have better firefighters because of the high risks involved. Firefighting has its downsides, including death and injury, which is why it is crucial for training officers to have the internal desire to develop their people. There are different ways to promote a firefighter's development. Availability is one way; training officers should be available. Their availability allows them to offer guidance and counseling services to the firefighters.

> "Developing others is <u>YOUR</u> responsibility."

Such services enable them to understand the firefighters' struggles, establishing the required remedies.

Training officers should listen to others. Many ideas presented by these firefighters are crucial for the department's development, making it essential that training officers be better listeners. Training officers should be consistent in their approach to the firefighter's concerns. A consistent approach builds trust between the firefighter and the training officer, allowing for a better relationship.

Lastly, training officers should want to make people better than them. To simply train their people up to a level below them is not only a disservice to their people but also to the public that it serves. Good training officers eat, drink, sleep, and breathe the desire to develop people; they seek constant improvement in themselves in their ability to instruct but also in how their people can continue to grow in their KSA's.

Ability to Inspire

A good training officer should have the ability to understand what makes people tick and use that to engage with them to establish buy-in. Training Officers should use their position to motivate others to achieve a common goal. Furthermore, they should inspire people to be better in their duties and set goals for their future growth in their fire service careers. Inspiration is a process that every aspiring training officer should follow.

It is human nature to want to be inspired. Many people wake up feeling like they have no purpose or lack the motivation to face the day. Firefighters are no different, throughout their fire service time they can lose their passion and desire for the job which proves their lack of inspiration. Therefore, it should be the responsibility of the training officer to change that attitude and that culture.

Training officers need to have the desire and the ability to motivate their people. If you are unable to inspire others, what are you really doing? The training officer needs to see what their people can be and not what they are. Firefighters are a unique bunch; in that they may put off the image that they are content in their current position or abilities. It is up to the training officer to have the ability to motivate those firefighters and show them what they can be. From there, it is also the training officer's responsibility to then establish the path for their people to grow.

Understand Sociology and Psychology

Different people have different learning capabilities, and the training officer should be cognizant of them as well as understand how best to manage those differences. Better management of their firefighters signifies better leadership. Furthermore, because of the behavior difference among firefighters, some will be impetuous, and there will be those who will be more relaxed. Impetuous firefighters will require more attention from the training officer because of their attitudes towards training and/or the organization, which can destroy the department's efficiency. A training officer with good leadership qualities will understand how to deal with such individuals because they understand psychology. By understanding personal psychology, a training officer can inspire them to be better in their activities. Having that ability to adjust the delivery of instruction or methodology in their program is vitally important for the success of a training officer.

On the other hand, sociology relates to studying human behavior about social change and life. A training officer should understand how to associate with the firefighters to allow better interactions. Better interactions allow for better training which is crucial for the firefighter's success rate. A training officer who understands the importance of developing a professional and positive relationship with their firefighters displays better leadership qualities.

Trial and Error

A good training officer should have experience that includes both successes and failures. They should understand that mistakes can make them a better firefighter and a better training officer. This explanation reintroduces the experience concept. Therefore, experience is the key to being a good training officer and a better training officer.

Without this experience, one cannot understand how it feels to fail or more importantly, the value of failing in their duties. Which therefore leaves them unable and insincere when attempting to teach their firefighters how to bounce back from such an incident.

The trial-and-error mechanism allows training officers to educate their firefighters on the value of not being afraid to make decisions without all the information or answers. Despite the odds of failing being remarkably high, it is an opportunity for them to grow and develop better ideas in the future.

Understand their Duties

Effective training officers should be fully cognizant of their responsibilities as well as dedicated to executing these tasks proficiently. Some training officer duties range from tasks that encompass guidance, mentorship, being a company representative, and undertaking various managerial duties. In the realm of the fire service, the training officer serves as a significant figure in training management, usually bearing an official rank. Their role necessitates not only fulfilling specific duties but also committing to the fire department's overarching goals and mission, with a strong emphasis on fostering personal and professional growth in others. While their main role is training firefighters, it should be understood that is an endeavor that demands meticulous planning and coordination to guarantee outcomes that meet established standards.

As stated earlier, a good training officer has had both the experience and education as a firefighter, driver/operator, company officer and encompasses good leadership which entails being a good follower of the rules making it essential that the training be efficient to allow for better performances. On the other hand, managerial activities include four essential activities, including **planning**, **leading**, **controlling**, and **organizing**. Training includes planning activities that the firefighters will perform in preparation for the season change. Early planning allows the firefighters to know their training, avoiding any confusion. Leading involves the training officer being the training's focal point and ensuring that the firefighters perform their duties accordingly.

Controlling relates to the training officer being in control of the training by providing that the firefighters look to them for guidance. Total commitment to the training produces better firefighters resulting in increased safety in the field. Controlling is the assurance that what was planned is completed and, in a manner, prescribed by the training officer.

Organizing ensures that the training occurs in an organized manner. A well-coordinated training program ensures efficient training because firefighters know what they are working on and how to accomplish their prescribed training. Furthermore, because different levels of training exist, the training officer should be able to organize their program to maintain the balance of the instruction needed to each firefighter's skillset. Such activity by the training officer makes them a better organized training officer and ensures program efficiency.

Position of Influence

A common misconception in society and especially in the fire service is that a position of rank is a position of power. Far too often people with rank fail in their responsibilities due to their misunderstanding that they have power. Human beings resist narcissists and egomaniacs who are obsessed with their rank and power and less focused on their ability to inspire and influence others.

It is important to understand that having a new role that has rank and responsibility should not be received as a position of power, but rather as a position of influence. Having the position offers you the opportunity to influence others. Being able to influence others, you can shape the future of your organization. There are several things that a training officer can do to influence those around them.

First, they should be optimistic about the results of their training. A training officer who is always negative about training instills the same mindset in the firefighters. This action ensures that firefighters develop less interest in training, making them inefficient in their duties. Such incidences are common in modern society because of the increasing pessimism among management. The proper establishment of an efficient training program should be of the highest priority for the training officer. A training program should comply with the firefighter's needs. While meeting those needs, it should suit the different demands that the firefighters should ensure that they offer their full compliance.

Lastly, training officers should understand what it means to be in their position. As Uncle Ben says to Peter Parker in Spiderman "with great power comes great responsibility." The training officer's position is influential because it provides the department's lifeline. Therefore, quite literally the department's services rely on the training officer to produce better and more proficient firefighters.

Networking and Team Building

Networking

Networking incorporates establishing mutually reliable and beneficial relationships with other agencies, businesses, or potential stakeholders. Networking is an essential skill that a training officer should possess because it allows them to be better facilitators. Better facilitators ensure that their relationships are both internal and external to their department.

These relationships can ensure that they acquire better training opportunities. For example, a good relationship with your local business owners can help ensure that the fire department receives good deals or donations on training materials needed to build training props which is both fiscally responsible and helps build those much-needed relationships with your organization's stakeholders.

Networking recognizes the need for the training officer to establish the amenities required for the fire department. For example, a good relationship with other training officers allows the organization to show what programs or equipment they may be missing in their training. Every day brings a learning opportunity, and the best way to learn is through networking. As the famous saying goes, *"those who want help should help themselves first."* Any training officer striving to be the best in their duties should acknowledge their downfalls and expose their own gaps and then seek a way to rectify them.

In addition, networking allows for training officers to gather information. Information exchange is crucial for any training officer because they get different training programs. Because networking brings diverse individuals together, training officers can improve their leadership and relationships with the firefighters. It presents them with the learning opportunity to extend their knowledge and experience on the job.

For example, one training officer can have skills that another training officer lacks. Networking provides the opportunity for them to teach each other how best to integrate their skills in training.

Lastly, this shows humility in the sense that you as the training officer do not have all the answers, but you are willing to find someone that can help you get there. Training officers who network also should network within their own organization. For example, some firefighters have a specific background or skillset that you as the training officer may not have. If there is a need for the team to train on that specific skillset, you should have that firefighter lead the way in the development and execution of that training topic. This proves the training officer's willingness to work with others but also helps build future leaders by giving them a task that gains responsibility and creates ownership. It is okay to not have all of the answers, but to at least be willing to ask someone for help.

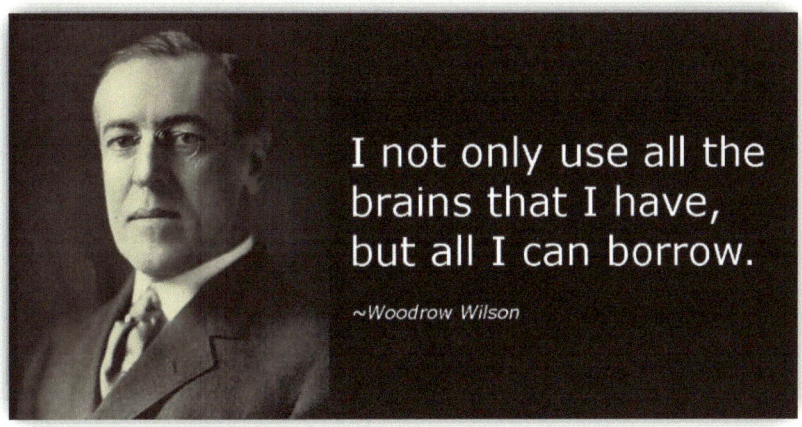

U.S. President Woodrow Wilson sums up the value of networking

Team Building

Where there is a training officer who is searching for efficiency, there should be different groups who help introduce new ideas into training. There are multiple levels of firefighters; therefore, there are multiple levels of talent and knowledge that can be implemented into your training program. For example, a new firefighter's skills may not be the same as those with more experience, therefore the senior firefighters can help improve your training program by offering their expertise to the newer firefighters. Because there will be different disciplines and priorities during the delivery of training. Assistance from experienced firefighters in the instruction of specific training disciplines will help develop cohesion amongst the crew and thus build a strong team.

Different people have more proficiency in various skills. One individual may be better at mechanical tasks, while another may be proficient in critical thinking. The training officer should establish how they can manage these individuals and ensure that their skills provide the best outcome for the fire department. Aligning their strengths can make a good team, especially in the field, because they understand the strengths and weaknesses of each other.

If the training officer wants to improve the team-building process, they should listen to others. The firefighters know each other well because they spend most of their time together. Because of this factor, it makes sense for the training officer to ask for assistance when forming teams from the firefighters. We will cover this in more detail in Chapter 7 "Building A Training Network."

"I Love You…Bye!"

Establishing an environment where there is room for fun while maintaining the "business" side is important. Whenever I get off the phone with any of my firefighters, I always end it with "I Love You, Bye!" Even if I am half-joking, I'm also half-serious. I shake things up by ending it with that off the wall comment, but I also mean it. They know that I appreciate them and love them like they are family. This is an important factor when trying to build a team, the team is like a family, they need to believe that they are a part of something in order to be willing to participate. In short, the training officer should motivate the firefighters to improve their training for better involvement. A training officer should not shy away from showing love to the firefighters because it boosts their trust, allowing for cohesion which leads to a strong team.

> *"Proper motivation includes leading by example and showing them love and support when they need it."*

Over the next few chapters, we will dive into more detail about some of the items discussed throughout this chapter. If you are already a training officer and weren't aware of or implementing some of the items discussed above, hopefully this book has already started to get your gears moving. If you are an aspiring training officer, hopefully this has started to paint a picture of the level of importance there is behind being a training officer. As we dig deeper, the intent is to offer you some nuggets of information coupled with giving you that gut-check moment of what it is that you are responsible for as a training officer.

A VIEW FROM EXPERIENCE

By: P.J. Norwood,
Director of Training Connecticut Fire Academy
Deputy Chief (ret.) East Haven (CT) Fire Department

P.J. Norwood is the Director of Training, CT Fire Academy. He is Retired Deputy Chief from the East Haven CT Fire Department; He has served four years with the CT Army National Guard. P.J. is a FDIC Instructor, Fire Engineering Advisory Panel Member, Fire Engineering book and video author. P.J. also serves on the UL-FSRI Technical Panel for the Study of Residential Attic Fire Mitigation Tactics and Exterior Fire Spread Hazards on Fire Fighter Safety. P.J. is a Public Safety Education Group advisory member for UL-FSRI. He is certified to the Instructor II, Officer III, Fire Marshal and Paramedic level.

The Training Officer

The most difficult position I held in the fire service.

When I was promoted to training, I was only 37 years old, with approximately 60% of the department having more time on the job. I was an outspoken firefighter who was never afraid to voice my opinion. I was never afraid to try something new, and I was never concerned about what others thought of me. I was a firefighter and paramedic, and I prided myself on being good and aggressive at everything I did. Looking back, I know now I was "lucky," and my skills, confidence, and the training I received from many kept me alive and relatively unscathed. I want to explain why the training officer role was the most difficult position I held in the fire service and offer some suggestions on how to survive. The TO role is not for everyone. It is not for someone who has thin skin or is worried about what others think. You will be put into situations to uphold the mission and vision of the Chief. At times, that vision may not be within your beliefs, but your job is to carry out his or her orders. Now, that is not to say you will not stand up for what you believe in and have a respectful and appropriate conversation behind closed doors with the Chief. However, when you leave that office, you need to follow the chief's directions.

Now, on the surface, this seems very easy. However, when you are delivering the message or training topic in a classroom, at the kitchen table, or on the training grounds, your firefighter will see right through you. Firefighters are the smartest people (at least most of them) that walk this earth, and if you are selling a bag of shit to them, they know it and will call you out on it. You cannot bullshit a Firefighter! If you do not know what you are doing, are below par with your skills, and have never done what you are trying to teach them, they will call you out for it. This leads to a lack of credibility and respect. With poor credibility and less than 100% respect, you will be completely ineffective. When the training officer is ineffective, people get hurt and can get killed in this business.

Do You Have What It Takes?

I began my career as a fire explorer in 1988 and joined the career fire department in 1995. I moved through the ranks and was promoted to Deputy Chief training officer in 2011. The department I worked for was a combination department that had a response staff of forty-four firefighters who operated three engine companies, one ladder truck, and one EMS rescue unit.

Our volunteer members comprised approximately one hundred members who operated four separate companies and responded on two engine companies and three EMS rescue units. The operations and administrative office were staffed by four individuals. The positions of Chief and Assistant Chief were non-union appointed, whereas the positions of DC of Training and DC of Fire Investigation were union appointed.

We covered 12.6 square miles and responded to an escalating call volume each year, approaching 5,000 in my last year before retirement. These calls came from our diverse district that included Long Island Sound, the Regional Airport, Interstate 95, a tank farm that stored jet, diesel, and home heating fuel, along with the normal working-class town filled with one-, two-, and three-story private dwellings, apartments, condominiums, light manufacturing, industrial, and hi-rise apartment complexes.

We responded to all the "normal" responses that many of your departments make each day. From fire to EMS to public service calls. We also had the unfortunate experience of Mother Nature with hurricanes, tropical storms, and blizzards. The firefighters were truly jacks of all trades. We did it all with minimal staff and, in the early days, poor equipment, and we did not always have the full support of the training division.

I mention the make-up of my department and the response district so you, the reader, can understand the environment I worked and operated in. I was the training officer and the designated safety officer. I operated a training division that included myself. I considered myself lucky when the Chief would approve overtime for some of the amazing firefighters and officers that were certified instructors to assist me with drills.

The other piece of added stress that can take its toll is the burden of the position. Every issue, problem, or mistake in a response can and will be, to some extent, blamed on training. Now, that is not to say every issue, problem, or mistake is the result of poor training. This is a heavy burden for some to bear.

Furthermore, it is inevitable that the firefighters under your command will get hurt. It is the nature of the business. You need to understand that all injuries cannot be prevented. If you are training to national best practices, consensus standards, adhering to all OSHA or other safety practices, and truly training, not just checking boxes by watching YouTube, you are doing your job, and injuries can and will still happen. Now, if injuries occur because of a lack of training, a lack of quality training, or a lack of injury prevention education, which is directly related to the training officer!

I mention this because it is critical for you to understand some of the downsides of the position. All too often, many officers do not want to discuss the negative aspects of promotions. Me, I would rather put it on the line and let you make an informed decision that is best for you, your family, and your career.

The role of training officer is also extremely rewarding.

After operating at a private dwelling fire where one of my firefighters became "trapped' on the second floor of a residential house fire, he had fire coming up the stairs and into the bedroom he was searching. He calmly closed the door and called for a ground ladder. Upon meeting up with him, immediately after he said, "Chief, thank you," Once I realized I could not go down the stairs, I remembered everything you told me. Stay calm, close the door, and call for assistance if necessary.

Sitting back and watching incidents unfold, you will see amazing acts of heroic effort unfold in front of you. As Chief Frank Leeb so eloquently put it following a major fire in the Bronx that took the lives of seventeen civilians and injured sixty "We reflect on the value of our members and their dedication."

We also reflect on their training, the foundational cornerstone that prepares and positions our members to perform under even the most demanding of conditions. "There were many heroic and amazing actions inside and outside the fire building by both fire and EMS members."

As the training officer, some but not all of that is in direct relation to the continued daily training your members receive. It is also a testament to their entry-level training and their individual commitment to both formal and informal training. However, days like those in the Bronx make you realize how training saves lives for both civilians and firefighters.

Looking back at my career, I would not trade any part of it, from firefighter, paramedic, battalion chief to deputy chief of training. Each position had its challenges, rewards, good days, and bad days. But, in the end, I would not go back and change anything. Change some of the outcomes, yes, of course.

As you climb the chain of command into training, you can impact every single member of the department and every single incident and event that the department responds to.

"Heavy is the head that wears the crown." Any person who has been in training knows the meaning of that statement.

You, your department, and the community you serve will daily reap the benefits of the training that is provided by the training officer. Do not take the training position lightly. Do not take a promotion to training for a pay raise, a better schedule, a higher rank, or bars on your collar. Accept a position in training because you want to work with the membership to have a positive impact on your community each and every day!

Chapter 2

Training Officers Are Leaders, Too!

If you are aspiring to become one or already are a training officer, first and foremost, you should know that by the very nature of being a training officer, you are a leader. This chapter is important because far too many times a person who has had no leadership experience takes on the responsibility of the training officer role and fails in the execution of their program.

Let's put it in the perspective of the training officer, if you are teaching a class, you are leading the room. Your students and firefighters will follow your instruction, providing that instruction is true and relevant. Training officers who either were poor leaders or never served in a leadership role often struggle as they take on the responsibility of the training officer.

Throughout the fire service, there has been a history where the training office position has been treated as a "stow-away" instead of as a true developmental opportunity. There are cases where some training officers got their jobs after failing to be efficient in their previous duty. These inefficient officers get into these training officer roles without sufficient experience in the field, creating issues within the training division. In the long run, firefighters fail to be efficient in their duties, which can increase the number of fatalities in the field. Because of this issue, fire departments should employ good training officers who understand the dynamics of their jobs and have a passion for training.

Leadership is the first quality that these officers should possess. Good leadership entails core managerial activities, including coaching, mentoring, and company officer duties. These duties are crucial because they determine the department's performance. Without these activities, the department cannot operate effectively. Therefore, the training officer qualifies to be the department's spearhead because of the crucial activities.

> *"First and foremost, you must know that by the very nature of being a training officer, **you are a leader**."*

Leadership Qualities of a Good Training Officer

A good training officer should have experience as a leader, however, to be a good leader one should have experienced the life of being a follower. They know what it means to be a good subordinate; therefore, they understand that leadership involves making good and tough choices. Leaders do not assume their positions straight away, but they grow into them naturally. Some of the components that make a good leader include:

Good Follower

Being as each training officer is in a position of influence and therefore serves their organization as a leader, they should have experienced what it was like to follow others before they attempted to lead. They, therefore, know how their firefighters from "the floor" may receive the different commands, and expectations demanded by the leader.

The importance off following before you lead.

The situation is no different for a training officer who should ensure that their firefighters are being trained and developed fairly. As a leader, I was once under someone else's leadership in the fire department. What makes a good leader and training officer is having first served as a good student of the fire service and a good follower of their leaders within their organizations. However, being a good follower can often be a double-edged sword. One should be cognizant of not becoming a blind follower. Blind followers in the simplest form to describe it is basically a "yes-person."

They lack innovation in their own ideas and despite their own conscious, they will follow a bad leader or perform in a training evolution for a less than adequate training officer simply to withhold the appearance of being a "desirable" member of the organization. Yes, there is a huge disparity between these two followers. For you to understand this concept, take a look at your own organization. Whether you are already a training officer or aspiring to be one it is important to have an understanding of what a blind follower is. Some people do everything their training officer or boss requests them to do regardless of whether the commands are right or wrong.

Sitting in traffic for no reason

On the other hand, some leaders are cautious in what they do, and they do not follow every command their training officer or supervisor gives. They can decipher between good or bad orders. They are the good followers by leading and evaluating the decisions they are making, while the others are blind followers. If you still cannot relate to the situation, look at this example. You are driving, and you decide to sit in traffic for no apparent reason. As a result, those behind you do the same thing without checking whether there is actual traffic on the road. Those who stopped their cars and sat in the traffic are blind followers. They follow what someone else is doing without looking at the big picture.

Despite this distinction between good and bad followers, I am not saying that you start questioning every decision your training officer or boss makes. This will result in you being a bad follower, manifesting in your leadership ability. Instead, take the initiative to question yourself and not the manager or the training officer. If you are uncomfortable with a specific directive, tackle it with your leader at an appropriate time or place. Such action is essential in ensuring respect between the leader and the subordinate, ensuring better relations.

Be A Good Subordinate

A good leader was once a good subordinate. Who is a good subordinate? Good subordinates respect authority, and just like good followers, know the boundaries between their leaders and themselves. Whenever they have an issue with a leader's rules, they do not question them publicly but wait for an appropriate time to raise their frustrations. Think about it, how would you feel if an employee questioned your rules publicly in front of every employee. It would be a sign that they undermine your leadership, resulting in disputes. Judging by my experience as a leader, I know that aggressive leaders may make life challenging for such firefighters, leading to an unwillingness to participate, being "checked-out," and eventually to their resignation, because people do not leave a job, they leave a bad leader. By being a good subordinate, one learns a clear boundary between authority and others, ensuring a better bond between them and their leaders.

Someone who was a good subordinate understands this concept, making them good leaders. First, as leaders, they will not put their firefighters in situations that make them vent and undermine their authority. Such traits are only available to those who were subordinates. This situation directly corresponds to the idea that leadership is more of a gradual process than a one-time achievement. If it were a one-time achievement, then everybody would be a leader. But it requires one to undergo significant development to be an effective leader. I will leave you with one question to ponder: think of a training officer, instructor, or leader that you had that was most influential on you. Do you think or possibly even know whether they were those who were good stewards to their organization and good subordinates to their leaders or were they those who inherited the role without being a subordinate? I would be willing to bet my salary that they were the former rather than the latter.

Command the Room

Training Officers should possess the ability to be authoritative figures with their people both in and out of their organization. They should take charge of the room and express a natural sense of being the leader of the situation. Firefighters will certainly undermine leaders who have no command presence because they feel more powerful than them. This same attitude applies to the learners or students. Firefighters will display no respect, nor regard for a bad training officer who lacks the ability to command the room and similarly command the training ground.

This situation brings about the question: Is leadership about rank or influence on others? The answer is the latter. The more a training officer influences others, the more they are likely to take charge of a room. Influencing others is not about providing harsh regulations but being fair and the correct mentor. Fairness in leadership brings respect. Many leaders in modern society confuse fear with respect. Fear may be an efficient way of creating order in an organization, but it forms minions rather than firefighters.

This illustration means that firefighters will follow you not because they respect you but because they should; otherwise, they face a potential disciplinary action. This type of situation can lead to a toxic work environment full of unsatisfied firefighters engaging in gossip and hatred. The long-term of such a situation is an uncoordinated workforce, which undermines the organization's productivity. Due to the training officer's lack of holding command of the room, the situation can become detrimental throughout the fire department, thus casting a shadow over the main task of providing communal safety. If firefighters are not properly training together and meeting the objectives set for each training discipline, they cannot offer the expected protection to the community caused by a lack of executing the training officer's assigned tasks during training.

Such a damning scenario is because of an ineffective leader who cannot command their firefighters. It is one of the essential leadership aspects, which has detrimental effects if a leader ignores it.

Don't be the Problem; Be the Solution

Firefighters should always look to their leaders for guidance. The more they see their leaders as their guidance, the more they see them as their solution. A leader who is aggressive and biased in their rules will never portray an image of being a solution to their firefighters. Firefighters will see them as a problem. Some may see them as the cause of an organization's failing. All these adverse incidents constitute a problem rather than a solution. As a leader, I recognize that I should attempt to be the beacon of hope to my people if I am ever to manage them successfully. Furthermore, it is my goal to create an atmosphere where every firefighter feels comfortable sharing their struggles with me. This openness ensures that my people see me as more of a solution than a problem.

Look at this concept in this manner, when are firefighters most productive? Is it when they feel free talking to their bosses about their issues or when they fear their bosses? Most would or at least should argue that it is the former. The point here is to establish an environment where you are building your department or organization. If your people are too afraid to come to you with real problems, you are failing to develop a progressive culture. If they only come to you to rat each other out, then you have yourself to blame for creating an environment more suited for the sewers than one that is supposed to be protecting the lives and properties of its community.

In other words, the leader becomes aware of their firefighters' situations. They can understand their peoples' strengths and weaknesses, giving them a specified treatment. Such leadership boosts an organization's efficiency because of the teamwork it creates. In a fire department, collaboration is crucial because it leads to more life and property safety. Creating this environment can only happen if those in charge understand their role as leaders and take the time to understand what their firefighters expect of them.

Values of A Good Leader

In my experience, I know that there are values that every worker wants their leader to have because it assures them of a comfortable working environment.

In my experience some of these values include integrity, passion, and humility. Let's break each one of these values down.

Integrity

Integrity is doing what's right even when no one is looking. Many leaders today are guilty of having integrity when the cameras are watching. They only care about the medals they get from people recognizing that they have integrity. It is a damning trait for a leader to have integrity when people are watching. Firefighters may never respect you because they know your true side. A good training officer should always do the correct thing every day to provide a good picture to those around them. Firefighters will look up to you because they know that you're not faking it.

Yes, it may sound harsh, but training officers should not be pretenders and simply "fake it, till they make it." Demonstrating a trustworthy image to the firefighters creates trust within the organization. Your people will feel more comfortable sharing their struggles with you because they know that you are genuine and not pretending, because you have proven and established an environment that shows you to be an honest person. This example shows that integrity leads to trust and openness between the training officer and the firefighters, resulting in workplace efficiency.

Passion

Another quote that has always stuck with me comes from Chief Lasky where he says, "a leader with passion but no skill will always outperform one with skill but no passion." The statement is true because the passionate leader will always fight for what they believe is right and do away with what they see as wrong. Despite this factor, you should understand that passion is a double-edged sword. On the one hand, passion means an intense desire for something, while on the other hand, it means an outburst of emotions, including anger. The latter description is one of the main downsides of passion. Therefore, leaders should know how to control their emotions and not react dismissively to their people because it shows a lack of professionalism.

Chief Rick Laskey,
Author of Pride & Ownership

A passionate training officer can avoid the downsides of passion by remaining open-minded. Being open indicates that they are ready for valid criticism about their proposals or better suggestions. Knowing how to manage your frustrations in such incidents shows that you are a good leader. Furthermore, training officers can avoid the negative side of passion by holistically seeing everything behind them.

Take an example of a chess game; a skillful player sees the game from every angle. As a result, they expect different moves that keep them ahead of their opponents. Giving a 30,000 foot "birds-eye" view helps them see the big picture.

This one-step-ahead approach helps them overall because they win the game rather than taking steps forward but losing a vital chess piece like a queen. This is the same when it comes to being strategic both as a leader and as a training officer. Good leaders are passionate, but they do not let passion take advantage of them. Instead, they are insistent on being open to other people's suggestions and integrating them into their strategies. After that, they can use that passion to ensure that the proper execution of the strategy is done efficiently and correctly.

Humility

A good training officer understands a clear distinction between pride and ego. These two words often get inter-used by people, leading to a poor justification of their actions. Having a zero-ego mindset ensures that one can bounce back whenever one hits rock bottom. U.S. Army General George Patton once said that "I don't measure a man's success by how he climbs, but how high he bounces when he hits bottom." It takes a person of true and actual character to show this trait because many people will give up after failing.

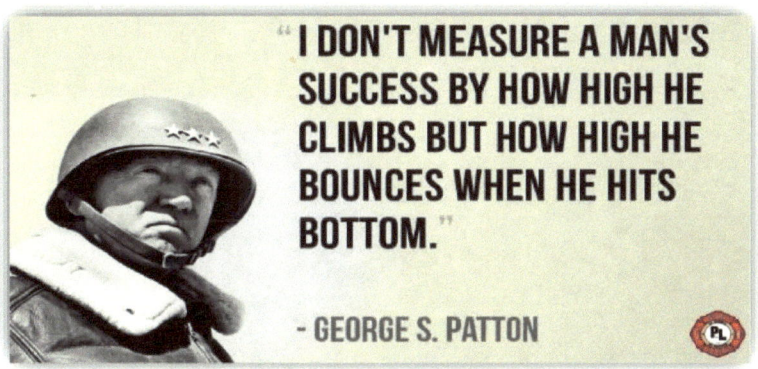

General Patton on Humility

Do You Have What It Takes?

A good training officer should have a strong commitment to their attitude because it directly reflects their personality and behavior to others. This behavior shows that they take pride in their character, which is different from having an ego. Ego makes people less likely to receive other people's suggestions, making them close-minded, a terrible trait for any training officer. By being close-minded you are simply in "tunnel-vision" and are incapable of seeing the world around you, literally making you subject to disaster. This trait is equally harmful to the production of your training program and to your people. If you are close-minded to any of their ideas or to any outside suggestions, you will quickly lose your following and your people will have zero faith in your ability to develop them properly. Thus, subjecting your program to an inevitable failure.

Furthermore, egoistic training officers can be perceived as selfish, narcissistic, and arrogant, which creates an uncomfortable working environment because the firefighters feel reluctant to talk to take direction from them. The more a training officer continues to have an egoistic mindset, the more the firefighters will see them as a problem and not a solution. This approach will lead to a toxic environment full of unsatisfied and angry firefighters. This style and attitude will only lead you to establishing zero credibility along with zero followers.

Avoiding such an attitude is important as a training officer because firefighters do not want to sit through a lesson feeling as if their instructor only cares about him- or herself and not on the development of those attending the class. This example is why it is extremely important to understand the value of being selfless and not selfish. One way to look at this approach is by examining the Titanic event. The Titanic was a ship that sank because it hit an iceberg. RMS Titanic's Captain Edward Smith. Captain Smith was on the verge of retirement, and the Titanic's sail was to be his last. When the ship hit the iceberg, Captain Smith had a chance to escape, but as the ultimate person responsible for that ship as well as the lives on it, he decided to stay with them on board in an effort to ensure that others had a chance of survival. This was a true sign of leadership that shows that zero-ego leaders care about others and not just themselves. They do not see the first existing route and run; instead, they remain calm and see the best approach to help others. That situation is authentic leadership and vital in the fire department.

Know Your People!

A good leader is aware of their people's personal information and uses it to manage them efficiently. A mentor of mine once asked me how well I knew my firefighters. He asked me whether I knew they had children, and I said yes. He then asked me whether I knew the children's ages, wife's names, and why they wanted to be in the fire service. My answer was no, and he then told me that a good leader knows their people personally. Being aware of such intimate details ensures that leaders handle their people differently but appropriately. We live in a society where everybody has their strengths and weaknesses. These differences make it complex to impose one leadership style on everybody because the style may suit one employee and be an issue to another. Training Officers should be aware of their people's strengths and weaknesses and define a leadership approach that may work for them.

This approach paints an excellent picture for the training officer and allows firefighters' productivity to improve, increasing the overall organization's efficiency. This trait is one of the most critical skills a leader can possess in a fire department. Take a look at the incident below:

Captain "A" knows that *Firefighter "C"* is struggling with family issues which has affected their performance. Because *Captain "A"* took time to understand *Firefighter "C's"* personal struggles and is aware of their weaknesses and strengths, they now know that the issue *Firefighter "C"* is facing may undermine their overall productivity. As a result, *Captain "A"* is able to deliver constructive conversation and offer corrective actions to *Firefighter "C"* because they know their personal struggles. This approach has enabled *Captain "A"* to be awarded *Firefighter "C's"* trust, therefore making it easier to come to a resolution for both parties.

Captain "A" shows their cognizant nature by acknowledging *Firefighter "C's"* family problems and giving them the support that they need to re-establish themself. A leader who was unaware of their people's personal lives could not care about their problems, demanding that they continue working and perform better, regardless of their situation. The former cares for their people and their well-being, by knowing their people, they have an advantage of being able to navigate through those "tough times" or hard conversations that every person in leadership will face.

The incident described above leads us comfortably back to empathy. The reality is that any of us at any time can face such a serious struggle in our personal lives, which will certainly influence our performance. Making tough decisions is part of any leader's regime, but they should show compassion to ensure that they keep their people engaged. Coming out as too aggressive or "uncaring" when making unpopular decisions may result in a toxic environment.

Vision

Visionary training officers will always try to bring out the best in their people. They understand that in order to accomplish a specific goal, all firefighters should be working to achieve that goal. As a result, they ask themselves what is the most progressive way that they can bring out the best in their people. The answer is simple, providing the best environment to be at their best while constantly looking towards how to improve and stay prepared for the future. Training Officers who are able to bring out the best in their firefighters have an easier time achieving the organization's goals because the overall firefighters' productivity improves massively.

Reflection Questions

There are four vital questions that you can ask yourself:

- What does leadership mean to you?
- Does rank mean that you are a leader?
- Why are leaders important in the fire service?
- How are Training Officers leaders?

My response to the first question is that leadership is about having the ability to influence others, fill any gaps, create a fun work environment, inspires others, and seek out the value in others. These key aspects define good leadership, making people want to work under a given leader. As you critically evaluate the question, incorporate elements that will bring out the corporation's long-term success. In order to answer the first question appropriately, assume that you are the leader, and one is asking why your leadership is essential in your organization. If creating this hypothetical scenario does not suit you, you can look at leaders within your organization or peer group and determine their key attributes that make you believe they are good leaders.

My response to the second question is that one does not need to have rank to be a leader. I believe that the best leaders are unofficial leaders. This statement means that the way one carries out one's activities defines one's leadership rather than the position they possess. Please look at your organization; it may be a rural, metropolitan city, career, or volunteer. Some people are not leaders but are role models to others because of how they carry themselves. Such people are unofficial leaders, vital in any activity because their ability to influence others positively allows for the effective running of the organization.

The third question, leaders are vital in the fire service because they control the chaos. As mentioned earlier, ineffective leaders are incapable of managing chaos, resulting in more problems, including property and life losses. I know you are probably thinking about how leaders control disorder in the fire department. It is straightforward and involves three actions: being a beacon of hope, inspiration, and the ability to calm others.

Let us look at one example that shocked the global news: the September 2001 attacks on the United States. The incident found America unprepared and left our citizens in fear. U.S. President George W. Bush, had to deliver a speech about the ongoing situation. Many firefighters of the Fire Department of New York (FDNY) were unaccounted for, which led to many firefighters from all over the country wanting to go and rescue their fellow firefighters. It was a tense situation that demanded someone who could react appropriately and calm the masses down. President Bush did exactly that by delivering an "off-the-cuff" response to the crowd of irritable firefighters who were in shock and questioning what was transpiring around them.

The firefighters heckled the President as he tried to deliver his rehearsed speech over the megaphone "we can't hear you!" to which the President went off script and replied from his heart "I can hear you and the rest of the world can hear you, and the people who knocked these buildings down will hear all of us soon."

This powerful response quickly calmed the crowd and the American people down, as it showed us that though we were down, we were not defeated. His address shows three aspects: a beacon of hope, a source of inspiration, and providing calm in a chaotic situation. Like President Bush, the key roles of leaders in the fire department are the beacon of hope, inspiration source, and ability to calm others in a chaotic situation.

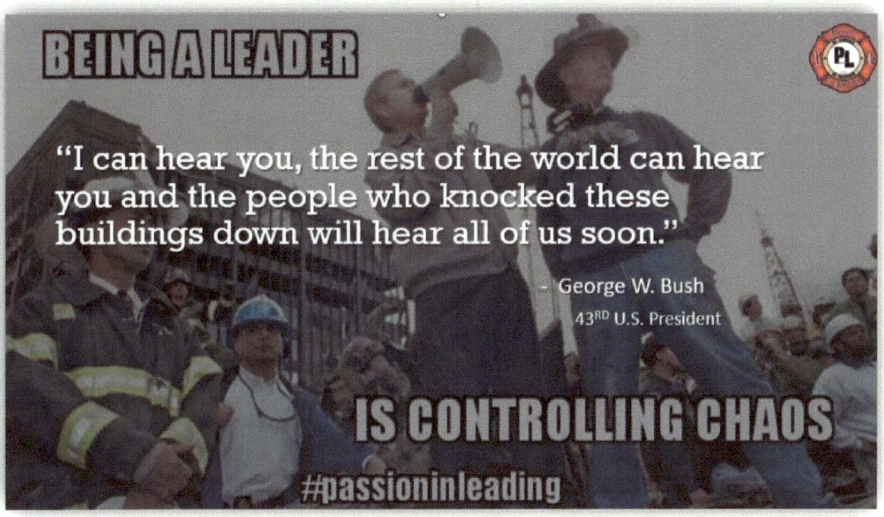

U.S. President George W. Bush on the scene of the World Trade Center attacks from 9/11/2001

As for the fourth question, as titled in this chapter and as you should know by now, training officers are leaders, too! Training Officers should have the ability to lead others, to inspire others, to coach, mentor and develop others. They are the pinnacle of what it means to be in a position of influence, due to the nature of their position and the responsibility that comes with that position. Training Officers are in the business of developing people, from the newest firefighter to the Fire Chief, it is the training officer's responsibility to establish the plan for developmental success for the people within their organization.

It is vital to keep in mind that you should think critically and evaluate each question independently when responding to these questions. There are different ways you can answer the questions, and it is not critical that you answer them the same way that I just did.

Bad Leadership

We have looked at good leadership, what entails good leadership, and the values that every good training officer should possess. It is only suitable that we also look at the other side of leadership and establish the traits that determine a terrible leader. By clearly distinguishing these sides, you can know which side you are on and decide whether or not it is appropriate to switch sides. My advice is you extinguish any of the styles discussed in this section because they undermine authentic leadership and create a toxic work environment. Furthermore, leaders having such traits in a fire department are part of why a fire department may fail to accomplish its duties effectively. Some traits of bad leadership include being close-minded, spreading gossip, abusing their power, creating hate/discontent or being indecisive. Let's look at these traits.

Close-Minded

Bad leaders think they are always right, and those around them hold no substantial feedback that could alter their opinion. It is a poor mindset for a leader, which creates dictatorial leadership. As a leader, you should set an environment where firefighters can raise their issues with a given policy. Ignoring such an essential bit of leadership ensures that firefighters see you as a dictator than a leader. Many of us know dictatorship is a leadership style that ends with strikes and protests.

Such actions in a workplace are unethical and could be prevented if a leader is more open to ideas and constructive criticism from those around him. Without the people to lead, leadership goes extinct.

Gossip

Leaders who gossip about their firefighters are toxic to the work environment. If you have a problem with your people, talk to them directly instead of gossiping about their failures. What benefit do you get from gossiping about firefighters? Nothing. You are creating a toxic environment where firefighters will refuse to share their problems because they are afraid of people making fun behind their backs.

As a result, it leads to a work environment full of firefighters facing mental issues, including stress and anxiety. Such a mindset is a recipe for disaster, especially in a fire department, because firefighters cannot perform essential functions in the field, jeopardizing lives, and property. Because these firefighters overthink every step-in order to prevent critical gossip, they lose the ability to manage their operations. After all, they fear their leaders gossiping about them and ridiculing them to other firefighters.

Abuse Their Power

Bad leaders use their power to benefit themselves and hurt firefighters. By hurting firefighters, I do not mean physical harm. In many instances, leaders formulate policies unsuitable for culturing a positive organizational culture. Abusive leaders also have zero empathy, immune to reasoning with their firefighters' issues. Organizations having such leaders cannot grow in the long term because many firefighters resign while others fail to reach their potential because of the poor work environment.

> *"Training should be meant for **Development** and not for Punishment!"*

An example can include a training officer who uses their power to set their firefighters up for failure, or worse to make a mockery of those who may be new or even nervous during certain training sessions. Training should be meant for development and not for punishment! The long-term impact on the fire department will be losing potential firefighters because of poor leadership. As a result, it makes it crucial that fire departments have a training officer who uses their power to encourage their firefighters, rather than abuse them.

Create Hate/Discontent in The Workplace

Most bad leaders do not create hate in the workplace immediately. It is a culmination of their ill-minded activities that make this situation. As a result, this hate in the workplace is a long-term effect of bad leadership. The activities that lead to this situation include gossip, being close-minded, and abusing power. Firefighters will see these things fostering and start developing negative emotions toward their leader. Those that have a good relationship with the leader will not be popular in the workplace because others will question why they get preferential treatment and not them.

As this poor culture fosters, it will be difficult to stop it because stopping it means you should do away with the current leadership. As a result, it leads to a situation where firefighters do not trust each other and see each other as why they get cruel treatment from their bosses. These trust issues are detrimental to a fire department because they limit firefighters' ability to save lives and property. The damning situation that emerges is the fire department's inability to assure community safety.

Indecisive

Bad leaders cannot provide definite results about any given judgment. Their indecisiveness puts the organization at risk because firefighters cannot respect someone who cannot give them direction. As mentioned earlier, firefighters look to their leader for a solution. In the case of indecisive leaders, firefighters will see their leaders as the problem because they cannot reach a decision quickly and lead them appropriately. In the fire department, indecisiveness is a bad trait because firefighters expect their leaders to make the tough calls. Any inability to make these tough calls comes out as weak, a character that will lead to firefighters undermining their leader in the future.

The point here is for you to have an understanding that being a training officer quite literally makes you a leader. Whether you are leading the classroom or running a drill on the training grounds… **you are leading** others. By the very nature of the roles and responsibilities of the training officer position, people look to you for guidance and development. If they do not trust nor feel the need to follow you, you will not be able to effectively design a program conducive to their wants and needs. It is important to be aware of this and to take the proper steps to bettering your abilities to lead others so that you can deliver a sound program to those who you are responsible for. Some of the attributes of both the good and bad leaders discussed throughout this chapter will now lead us into discussing some of the challenges the training officer may face, which we will continue in the next chapter.

A VIEW FROM EXPERIENCE

By: Jim Moss,
Captain Metro West (MO) Fire Protection

Jim Moss is a fire captain and paramedic for the Metro West Fire Protection District in St. Louis County, Missouri. His fire service passions include leadership, training, and mentorship. Along with Chief Dan Kerrigan, Jim is the co-author of the #1 Amazon Bestseller: *Firefighter Functional Fitness* and the author of *Firefighter Success: 20 C's to Firefighter Excellence*. Jim is a contributor to Fire Engineering Magazine and FirefighterToolbox.com. He has shared his message at FDIC, Firehouse, the International Society of Fire Service Instructors, the National Volunteer Fire Council, International Association of Fire Chiefs, and nationwide.

The 3 I's of Leading as a Training Officer

If we were to boil down leadership to its most fundamental purpose, it always comes back to our ability to achieve the three I's: *influence, inspire, and impact.* As training officers, our mission directly aligns with these three I's.

Influence

Being a training officer goes hand-in-hand with leading others because we must use our position to positively influence others to become better than they were yesterday. The training officer who is leading effectively will use their competence and credibility to influence their firefighters to real change and real improvement.

How can we build our level of influence with those we are training? It's pretty simple: know the material forwards and backwards, know our audience, keep training simple and short, and know what kind of delivery method works best for our students. If we consistently do these four things with our training sessions, we will gain respect and credibility, which will increase our level of influence. The more influence we have with our people, the more we can help them achieve (and expand) their potential.

Inspire

As training officers and leaders, we should use our charisma to inspire our firefighters with a passion for training and self-improvement. Let's be honest: every firefighter wants to be inspired, and they want to be led. They might not all admit it, but deep down every firefighter likes good training. However, if our firefighters aren't necessarily excited to train, we need to examine why and address the issues that need fixing. Maybe their past training lacked the 3 R's: *relevance, realism, and repetition.* Or perhaps the previous training officer was "over-training" them—possibly expecting an unrealistic level of perfection.

We must remind our firefighters (and ourselves) that we are all striving for excellence and progress, not perfection. We won't achieve perfection every time, but if our goal is excellence, then we have the right mindset moving forward. Lastly, one of the most important ways we can inspire others is through our own passion. Just like almost everything else in life (attitude, behavior, etc.) our passion is contagious! Let's show up to training with excitement and energy, ready to inspire our fellow firefighters—they will take note and feed off our charisma.

Impact

Lastly, we must remember that the training officer is in the perfect position to make a positive, lasting impact on our fellow firefighters. When a firefighter is in the middle of training and everything "clicks" for them, we make a tangible impact on the way they think and how they perform—not only in training, but also on the fireground. How can we make more of an impact with our training? First, we must communicate the "why" behind the skills, strategies, and tactics. Firefighters want to understand why the information that we are communicating to them is important. They want to know that their training is 100% relevant and applicable to real-world firefighting. When we take the time to help them understand the "why," we create better buy-in, which begets greater self-investment, and yields a maximum impact. After they know the "why", the "what" and the "how" easily fall into place.

As training officers, let's never forget how we influence, inspire, and impact those we train. Let us not forget that the position provides us with an amazing privilege: to lead others to become the best that they can be.

Stay fit, Stay safe.

Chapter 3

Challenges for the Training Officer

Budget

Let us begin by describing what a budget entails in the fire department. Every fire department should deliver a budget to the appropriate committees to handle activities like training and essential travel.

Some of you may find it astonishing that fire departments require travel in their training budget. Yes, they need to include travel and professional development training as a line item or expense because of sending firefighters away to training provided in a specified area outside the local fire department's area.

Because of this, it is imperative to include the opportunity for your firefighters to attend training outside their local response area.

This situation not only helps offer the ability for your people to attend courses that you may not have available within your area, but it also allows them to gain a broader perspective on the topic. When you send your people to courses offered through an outside agency, this can help our people see things that they may not have been aware of within their response areas.

Another added benefit to sending people to attend courses or training offered through an outside agency is requiring the attendee to develop a summarized version of what they learned upon their return. This situation allows our people to learn new strategies without bias, but it is also cost-effective for our budgets. By sending one or two people to these types of training, they can now pass on the information gained to our 30 or more people. So therefore, in theory, we have now been able to train new concepts to our entire team at the cost of sending only two people. Fire departments face budget cuts, which could be detrimental to their training needs.

The responsible committees' "bean-counters" may indicate that specific training needs may be unneeded and/or ineffective, forcing training officers to make cuts and remove particular training needs to save money. As a result, the training officer faces the significant challenge of ensuring that the firefighters are still obtaining the training requirements and able to meet the mission needs. Many organizations cutting these budgets have zero clue which training is vital and could potentially lower the skillset, putting the community and firefighters at risk. This result puts maximum pressure on the training officer because they have to work with training that may not be effective for firefighters in the field.

The situation ensures that training officers lose desire and momentum in the progressive development of their training program. This loss is because they feel that all responsible bodies under-appreciate their work, leaving them with limited resources needed to deliver an efficient program. A training officer with minimum passion and momentum is likely to spread a similar feeling to the firefighters, making the fire department ineffective in their operations. Overall, community safety is at risk because of the fire department's loss of work desire and momentum.

You may be asking yourself the recommended way of budgeting. The answer is zero-based budgeting. Zero-based budgeting is a technique that involves creating a new budget from scratch instead of using previous budgets as a starting point. Furthermore, the method allows those who work on the budget to investigate all departments and indicate what they will need for the next financial year. As a result, any increase in the budget will have a justification because each budget component will have its related costs. This situation will ensure that budget cuts and increases are justified because any costs will have an appropriate justification.

How to Budget Efficiently

Complacency is a common issue in many fire departments. Many fire departments use previous budgets to create the following year's budgets. This activity is a poor way of budgeting because it does not present the department's costs. As a result, the budget increase has zero justification because it includes unnecessary annual increases. This situation leads to budget cuts, a condition that impacts the training quality in fire departments. If a carryover style of budgeting is used it is important that the budget managers evaluate the expenses from the previous year and determine if those expenses need to continue, the project has been completed or an increase is needed to complete the programs goals.

What to Consider Before Budgeting

Some of the questions that the department heads should ask themselves before starting a new budget are:

- Is there equipment or materials that are needed to meet the mission needs?

- What is the status of training props on hand and whether they require updating, building or replacement? This question will ensure that training officers break their training into different sections, including fit testing, ladder testing, pump testing, hose testing, and perishable training materials like hay and plywood. All these sections relate to compliance.

- Will there be overtime costs (if you are a career department or running a fire academy)? Certain compliance requirements and training needs may create overtime, something the budget should consider. Training related to compliance may also include annual SCBA training, quarterly structural firefighter training, and general training for officers and command staff.

- When a department is operating a recruiting class or if they are moving their recruits to a different training location the training officer should consider the financial impacts and plan accordingly. Both off site training locations and the overall academy have significant budgetary costs. For example, operating a recruit class impacts overtime and staffing, while fees and books impact both situations.

- Are there enough funds to support training needs to secure the mission's requirements? The training committee should inform the appropriate jurisdiction about any potential impacts to the organization's service delivery capabilities incurred by the training budget. Constant communication will ensure that the "bean-counters" are more considerate in budget allocations. The training team should avoid a scenario where they only meet the policymakers when they have faced a budget cut.

- The training committee should consider asking for more than ask for less. If there is a budget cut and the committee has asked for less, the allocated amounts towards training will be impacted, which can result in poor quality of the training needs because of the lack of available funds needed to pay for classes, books/learning materials and maintain or update equipment that is needed for training.

- Do budget cuts only affect the fire department, or do they also affect society in the long run?

- What is the primary cause of ineffective department operations?

- Does the budget impact career progression training opportunities (leaving you vulnerable to a broken succession plan)?

Documentation

Documentation is critical in fire departments because it captures what they are training on and the types of emergencies they respond to. Proper documentation allows the training officer to reference the frequencies and types of incidents the fire department has a mission for in their routines. By reviewing both training and incident reports, the training officer has the framework of the mission needs and the fire department's service delivery capabilities. Service delivery capabilities are how proficient and adequately equipped the fire department is so they can respond to and provide the services needed for their response areas.

Proper documentation can also provide a solid argument when attempting to secure or justify required funds from the budget. Another example of the importance of good documentation is if your fire department is seeking accreditation through agencies like the Commission on Fire Accreditation International (CFAI), where proper record keeping, and documentation are crucial in successfully assessing your fire department. However, training officers should consider the most critical reason for appropriate documentation would be in the unfortunate event of facing a legal review. For example, Insurance companies or even the National Institute for Occupational Safety and Health (NIOSH) may request to see the training documents if someone gets in an accident. A fire department with zero documentation will likely face liability because it is a negligent act that risks community safety. A training officer should always ensure that the training activities are on record to avoid personal liability and comply with the fire department's regulations.

The Occupational Safety and Health Administration (OSHA) is a volunteer program that is not dependent on the state. It can also offer framework for fire departments to implement into their safety procedures and used as a guide. Another example can be the National Fire Protection Association (NFPA). The NFPA can also be a great tool when looking for standards to reference. Many States and U.S. providences and territories including Puerto Rico and the Virgin Islands incorporate OSHA for their fire department safety standards. Below are some of the states within the US who may use OSHA.

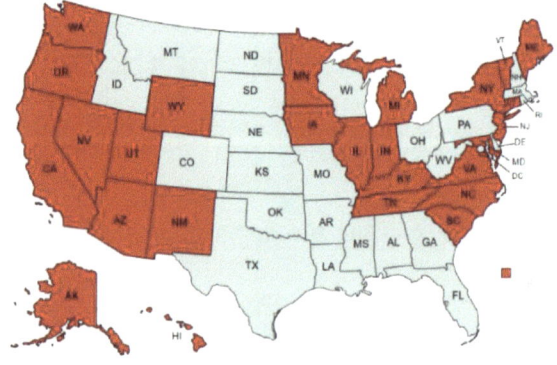

OSHA regulated states (in red)

OSHA also offers free consultations on safety recommendations and training suggestions. The hidden secret here is that if you invite them to your organization to do an assessment and/or consultation, they cannot hit you with violations or fines because you are taking the active steps of exposing any potential threats so you can build a plan to correct and/or prevent them.

One challenge training officers may face is the redundancy that some documentation incorporates. As a result, some personnel may avoid doing documentation because they find it unnecessary. Despite their purest intentions, if an accident were to occur, they may subject to facing personal liability, and at times, the liability crosses over to the fire department.

Practical Situation

While responding to an emergency, a firefighter operating the ladder truck accidentally hit a civilian car, leaving the driver (father) and his two children dead. The only surviving victim is the passenger (mother). The situation is horrible, but I will explain the importance of having proper documentation. When the insurance company and/or the lawyers start their investigations, the first thing they will request is the training documentation. A training officer with zero documentation could face significant charges along with the firefighter driving the ladder truck. If sufficient documentation were kept, this would assist in proving that the firefighter was adequately up to date with their required training and help the specific certifications and/or credentials qualify them as the ladder truck driver. This outcome could make it easier to manage the situation in a way that may protect the fire department, the training officer, and the firefighter. It would be valid considering that the driver was not negligent or driving under the influence.

I know the story appears extreme and possibly "one-sided" in favor of the fire department. I use this example because it perfectly illustrates why documentation is vital. Training officers should therefore integrate documentation into their routines despite their perceived redundancy.

Unions

Different unions represent fire departments throughout the world. Unions have multiple functions that assist in good program development and the organization of fire departments. Some essential actions that a union may take could be ensuring fund availability, better training, and ensuring that the proper amenities and resources are available to the fire departments. These functions keep the organization running and can help provide better training. One could argue that the unions are good because of the roles they deliver to their fire department. The answer to your thought is yes and no. Yes, because they provide the functions, and no, because they can also interfere with the overall department's operations.

Some unions may demand changes that may be ineffective in a department's operations. For example, some firefighters may refuse to go and participate in training drills if the temperatures outside seem too hot. In contrast, others appear to have the attitude of working as little as possible while demanding to be paid as much as possible. These examples can lead to the training program being subject to failure, resulting in unprepared and untrained firefighters. If the training officer insists on them training in such conditions, the firefighters may report to the unions because they see it as harassment. Some unions may be irresponsible and see the behavior as inappropriate and demand changes.

The situation makes training officers unable to handle their activities because of the laziness these unions instill in the other firefighters. This interference by the union within the fire department may appear to be a significant concern to training officers. As a result, they should be more professional and not allow their emotions to get the best of them when dealing with these challenges. The training officer has a duty in management to ensure that the contract does not hinder their operations. If the contract is a hindrance, the officer should not violate it unilaterally. Instead, the officer should work to ensure that the management drafts new terms for the next contract. Applying this initiative ensures that there are zero costly grievances.

Recruitment and Retention

Recruitment and retention can be significant issues in any organization. A fire department may find itself in a situation where it is hard to get people, or worse it is hard to keep their current members. Due to this situation, a continuous cycle may develop that can hinder the proficiency of any training program's success.

A problem that training officers may face is an increase in the having to frequently train inexperienced firefighters because of recruitment and retention concerns. Whether you are a volunteer or a professional training officer, you may face these challenges, making it difficult for you to ensure the proper proficiency training is being accomplished.

One example of a challenge the volunteer training officer may face is that their membership may not be able to commit to the training needs and other requirements fully. Their inadequate commitment is not intentional because many work full-time careers or have two jobs and will need to rest between their shifts. While others may have other vital obligations, such as families, coaching etc., making them forgo training to ensure that they fulfill those other responsibilities.

The situation makes it challenging for training officers to plan because they do not know how many people will turn up for training. Without sufficient training the personnel are not ready to efficiently respond to emergencies, which can result in reducing community safety because of the few numbers of proficient firefighters. The problem with recruitment and retention also lies with the department's culture. If the training officer is ineffective in their training, some firefighters may refuse to continue with the training and opt for other activities.

Test Your Understanding

Culture becomes a crucial aspect of the fire department and the training program. A positive culture can make recruitment and retention easier than a hostile culture. A positive culture involves members having a greater sense of belonging, while a negative one involves inappropriate workplace behavior like ego and abuse. Thus, subjecting your organization to people leaving it and in the fire service, words travel fast. As people go, they may pass on to others that they would not recommend your organization due to their negative experiences while there.

1. Who is majorly responsible for the firefighter's mood in training?
2. What can training officers do to ensure they have contented and happy firefighters?
3. Are recruitment and retention a vital concept in fire departments or a myth?

Annual Requirements

Many fire departments indicate their frustrations with annual requirements because many are redundant and unrealistic. Examples include new education requirements and new training regulations that may list topics such as conducting six to twelve structural drill requirements annually. These regulations may be what the appropriate bodies demand that training officers ensure that their firefighters complete.

The issue with certain training requirements is that training officers may find them ineffective for their training program. This judgement is justified because the training officer is the person responsible for developing a program that meets the mission's needs. The training officer is the one who is intimately engaged with their people and the efficiency of their program. They constantly evaluate and assess the productivity, skillset, and readiness of the firefighters responsible for responding to emergencies. If there are training requirements that have nothing to do with the mission, this may divert valuable time and attention away from productive training. That can create a situation where the firefighters start to not take training seriously because they recognize that they are investing time into something that does not develop their proficiency as emergency responders. Bottom line, the training officer has the best understanding of which training is good or bad.

In this situation, the main challenge the training officer may face is maintaining discipline and keeping their "game-face" so they can still train their firefighters without showing their reluctance to the training demanded by those annual requirements. A show of less concern is essential in ensuring firefighters become unresponsive to the training.

As a result, they should be professional in managing their training by indicating that the training officer agrees that the training may seem redundant while ensuring that all firefighters commit to completing it.

Training officers know which training is applicable in the field, making them responsible for formulating a solution to ensure its success. They should not just conduct "check-in-the-box" training. By "checking the box", it becomes negligence, which may lead to fatalities in the field. They should be reasonable enough to know that some training is unreliable and that their incorporation is mandatory among firefighters.

A training officer briefs their firefighters about the upcoming annual requirements the firefighters should participate in. These annual requirements are not typical to what may be considered fire and emergency services specific topics and can be more tedious or "check-in-the-box" computer-based training. While briefing this, the training officer openly expresses their disapproval of said annual requirements and then claims them to be unnecessary in front of the firefighters. Furthermore, the training officer then refers to the requirements as "stupid" and as a "waste of time."

Test Your Understanding

What effect is the training officer's reaction likely to have on the firefighters?

1. Firefighters have more motivation to work and train
2. Firefighters have less motivation to work and train
3. No effect

The answer will certainly be "2" the effect is that the firefighters have less motivation to work and train. Though there will be times where new training requirements may seem redundant or not conducive to the development of the firefighters, a good training officer should know that they are still a leader and in a position of influence. Meaning that, their opinion on matters can be perceived as the standard and therefore their people will also use that attitude as justification to not take the training seriously either. A training officer is an educator responsible for providing firefighters instructions. Good educators do not let frustrations get the best of them; instead, they remain calm and provide their duties professionally. The more they do this action, the less likely they may affect the firefighters with a negative attitude towards training and work.

Scheduling Conflicts

Weather Issues

I live in the Northeast, where the saying "the most consistent thing is the inconsistency" remains true when referring to the weather. It could be clear skies and 60 degrees in February, and suddenly, the next day, a snowstorm and 22 degrees! These unpredictable weather patterns make scheduling organized training a challenge because the training officer cannot plan which drill to include at a given time. As a result, advance scheduling is difficult, making many firefighters unable to plan how their training will affect the rest of their daily activities.

Emergencies

In other cases, a training session may be going as planned. The weather is excellent, and all firefighters are available for the training. Despite fulfilling the planned activities, an emergency comes up like a working fire, forcing all available personnel to go and respond to the incident. In such cases, the challenge lies with the training officer to ensure they find a viable solution to the scheduling conflict. Suppose the scheduled training focused on disciplines such as hose stretching or pump operations, and the firefighters who responded to the fire ended up performing those operations.

In that case, the training officer could use that as a credit to those specific tactics. The training officer could conduct an after-action with the firefighters who responded and host a table-top/question-and-answer scenario about the incident. This activity opens the dialogue to pointing out the things that went well while exposing what they may need to improve. What better way to ensure good scenario-based training than a real fire? This outcome not only helps the firefighters gain experience but also establishes a learning lesson for them to build from, thus continuing their development.

Staff Conflicts

Because many fire departments also have volunteers as firefighters, it becomes challenging to plan for training sessions because volunteers may have other pressing obligations. The lack of consistency on how many volunteers may show up to the scheduled training can subject the training officer to canceling the training. The potential of the reduced number of people available for training sessions could impact productivity, especially if the training requires a specified number of people to be effective. The potential risk involved with this challenge is the readiness of the firefighters due to being improperly trained or proficient in the needed skills and could subject the community to inadequate fire protection.

This challenge is also prevalent within the professional fire departments. While a training officer may attempt to be transparent and progressive by posting the upcoming training events a month or more in advance, this may result in some firefighters calling in sick on the training day. While the training officer should ensure that all the active members within their organization are being adequately trained and that all assigned training is fair and adequate, this can pose a significant challenge to maintaining the organization of the training program.

Due to the lack of participants needed to stand up for a training exercise, the level of proficiency and proper instruction required for a successful drill could fail. This situation can also affect the morale of the members, who end up having to pick up the slack caused by the absence of others, which can lower their motivation and desire to train at 100% effort in the future.

Meetings

Every employee has a boss, and every boss (probably) wants to have a meeting, and typically those meetings are on when the boss finds it convenient for their time. As a result, training can be scheduled for today, but suddenly the training officer receives a call from one of the chiefs that they should attend a meeting. As a result, if there were zero measures in place, the training could fail to happen. This situation is prevalent today because of the increasing number of redundant meetings.

A Training Officer should do the following to prepare for such scheduling conflicts:

- Remain optimistic and plan for the training regardless of the possibility that a scheduling conflict may happen.

- Have a backup plan in case one of the scheduling conflicts occurs. For example, if the bosses call the training officer for a meeting, the training officer should have someone else to oversee the training.

- Practice rescheduling. Rescheduling indicates that the training officer is more flexible, a trait that defines a good training officer. For example, if the weather interferes with the training, the training officer should be ready to call off the training and schedule it for another day. A similar situation applies to staff conflicts. This is why the training officer should be ready to reschedule the training to a day when many members are available to train.

A Global Pandemic

During the pandemic, the media and politics were significant forces that drove the situation among people in the workplace. As a result, it became prevalent that different organizations had to formulate new strategies to ensure that they meet the demands stipulated by the World Health Organization (WHO). One mandatory demand was avoiding contact with others. The situation led to several issues in fire departments when it comes to training. Many departments experienced training issues, course cancelations and attendance issues, laziness, declining levels of engagement and webinar usage.

Training Issues

The training was difficult to undertake because of the directive by the WHO to practice social distancing. Training in fire departments is a physical and interactive activity, and social distancing makes it complex to achieve it.

Ask yourself this question: Can American football happen with social distancing protocols? The answer is no, which is why all sports failed to happen when the pandemic started because they are activities requiring physical contact to be effective. This example is similar to training in fire departments, which requires the same physical contact for firefighters to understand its importance.

Social Distancing Caused Impractical Training Evolutions

Course Cancellations

Because of the closure of many educational institutions, there were increased course cancellations because it was impossible to offer them during the pandemic. Many firefighters were unable to finish courses that they were enrolled in, while others may not have had the opportunity to start the required classes they needed. As a result, this created a massive backlog in the number of courses and students waiting to be trained. This situation is one that many fire departments are still working towards bouncing back from which caused a potential regression in skills or sadly some have yet to even to address this setback.

Class Cancellations Due to Pandemic

Issues in Students Attending Classes

The closure of schools led to many classes going online. The situation is not practical for everyone; some fail to attend these classes because of poor connectivity and lack of Information Technology (IT) devices like laptops and computers. These issues in class attendance make it difficult for training officers to teach because of the failure to achieve the required quorum to continue teaching.

Laziness

The pandemic introduced a new behavior in fire departments with zero physical contact training. The situation made many firefighters complacent, complicating the training officer's duty. Apart from ensuring that the firefighters have the proper knowledge and skills for training, training officers had to ensure that their firefighters were not lazy because of the increased complacency.

Drilling through Webinar Classes

Conducting effective firefighting drills through webinar proved impractical and, at times, impossible to meet the needed intent of the curriculum. Not only did this method make it impossible for the training officer to supervise the firefighters participating in the training entirely, but also because the firefighters were not genuinely able to conduct the hands-on practical skills that are a valuable part of the lesson. As a result, the drills conducted through webinar proved ineffective, making those practicing them unprepared for what was to occur in the field. The situation is why many firefighters had to redo their drills when some restrictions were lifted, and we have attempted to get back to "normal."

Impracticality of Drilling Through Webinar

Zero Engagement

Because of the increased complacency among firefighters, there was zero engagement in training, a situation that made training ineffective, especially if the training officer depicted the same behavior. These challenges are a result of when the pandemic first started; more recently, we have been faced with a level of regression in the skills of our firefighters caused during the early stages of the pandemic. This situation has made it a priority for training officers to ensure that many firefighters return to basic skills and physical training. Because of the absence of such training, it is normal human behavior to become complacent and have zero engagement in training.

If the situation remains unchanged, training officers have a massive problem because the firefighters with zero engagement may affect others with the same behavior. A training officer should therefore take the appropriate steps to resolve this type of situation. Reintroducing a "back to the basics" training program is warranted and (probably) much needed. By doing this, the training officer can help their firefighters become reengaged in training and refresh their knowledge, skills, and abilities to perform proficiently.

Personal Agenda

Personal agenda involves having desires and motives that will only benefit oneself. It is a direct hindrance to openness and transparency in fire departments. This issue affects training officers and firefighters.

Let us first look at how the issue is a significant challenge for training officers; then, I will address how it may affect the firefighters.

Personal Agenda Among Training Officers

Training officers are the educators and those charged with ensuring that firefighters receive practical training. The challenge with this situation is that some may have a conflict of interest and decide to sabotage training to get more time or resources.

For example, if the training officer is focused more on their own personal agenda and development and less on what is best for the organization, the training will become inadequate. In many cases, training officers with personal agendas jeopardize training by ensuring they fail to teach all requirements demanded by a training session. What happens later is that firefighters become ineffective in their duties and may compromise community safety.

In such a scenario, the training officer is to blame because he or she let his or her agenda influence his or her duty to provide quality training. As a result, the training officer should be liable for those mistakes to ensure that similar occurrences do not repeat themselves.

Personal Agenda Among Firefighters

Many firefighters, to include the volunteers, may refuse to show up for training because they do not value what encompasses a good firefighter who loves the job. In some cases, there can be an attitude that because they are volunteers, they think it is okay to show up when they feel like it and not when necessary. Such a situation makes it difficult for training officers to issue proper training because of the inadequate personnel. In both scenarios, the training officer faces a challenge. I have witnessed this challenge throughout my tenure as a training officer with both career and volunteer firefighters.

Handling the issue requires a calm approach to avoid yelling at people for this attitude and their lack of willingness to participate in training. Framing things in a way that helps them understand how crucial firefighting is makes them see things positively, allowing them to have a better respect for the training and the fire service.

Coordinating Firefighter Safety and Resources

Firefighter Safety

Firefighting is a risky job that does not guarantee a safe return for those in the field. The situation makes it a challenge for training officers because they are responsible for providing the best training while ensuring their firefighters are safe both on the training ground and in emergencies. A case where the training officer provides inadequate training can result in poor performance by firefighters leading to increased injuries or possibly fatalities.

Test Your Understanding

A training officer is conducting a drill to manage emergencies in the field. The officer trains them on using different equipment but fails to teach them to handle their emotions in such emergencies. While operating at a fire a flashover occurs and then the second-floor collapses into the first floor. Firefighters on scene know that a member of their crew was on the second floor when this happened. While the incident commander and the rest of the crews pivot and formulate a plan to deploy the RIT or (FAST) team, one firefighter takes it upon himself to run in attempting to save his fellow firefighter. As a result, that firefighter and the one who was involved in the collapse both lost their lives.

In such a scenario:

1. Was the death of the other firefighter avoidable?
    a) Yes
    b) No
    c) None of the above
2. Who is responsible for the firefighter's death?
    a) The firefighter
    b) Training officer
    c) Incident commander
    d) Both b & c

The answer to the first question is yes. If the firefighter had been better trained, they would have known that there may be a limited chance to save the firefighter because of the underlying circumstances.

"At the cost of few, many were saved."

Two examples of this scenario can be referenced from the Worcester Cold Storage Fire, which tragically took the lives of six of our brothers. During the incident Chief McNamee made the decision to stop sending additional members into the building to locate 6 who were lost. Had Chief McNamee not made the unpopular decision to stop his members from continuing their interior efforts, they could have possibly lost more than six that night.

Another example is the fictional character of *Captain Jack Aubrey* (played by Russell Crowe) in *Master and Commander: The Far Side of the World.*

In the movie, there is a battle scene while at sea, a member of Captain Aubrey's navy falls overboard; if Aubrey were to turn the ship to save this one sailor, he would undoubtedly subject the rest of his crew to being hit with cannon fire and overtaken during the battle. Captain Aubrey's decision to retreat and leave the overboard sailor behind was not easy but proved that the situation justified his choice of action. At the cost of few, many were saved.

The answer to the second question is "d" Both b & c. If the training officer had trained the firefighter in handling such situations, the firefighter would have a better education and understanding of what risks were presented. As a result, the training officer's training would make the firefighter make better judgments in the field. In addition, the incident commander is equally at fault, having a better grasp of the span of control and maintaining proper accountability could have prevented this firefighter from freelancing and thereby running in.

Agency Resources

With the increasing budget cuts in fire departments, it is challenging for training officers to coordinate agency resources. Inadequate coordination leads them to low-quality training because of the insufficient amenities required to present the best training. Moreover, they cannot take their firefighters to train in other locations because of the limited available resources.

Having an understanding of good networking skills and a willingness to reach out to other agencies outside of your organization can be one way to help fill that gap. Bottom line, just because your agency may not have the resources available to support the training, does not mean you shouldn't train. A good training officer should find a way to secure quality training.

Egos

Just like personal agenda, egos affect training officers and firefighters. The training officer deals with different people in the class. Primarily, there is one category of people the training officer may encounter: They are what I have categorized as "The "know it all's." They are destructive to others because they undermine the training officer by showing off their knowledge and skills to others. It is okay to have better knowledge and skills than the training officer. What defines a good student is the ability to be respectful of the training officer's duty and not to make their training difficult. Many "know it all's" are inattentive in class, a behavior that may manifest in others if the training officer does not rectify the situation. As a result, the question that arises is how the training officer tackles the situation.

> *"Take the **E** out of EGO and **Go** be **E**ffective."*

How To Handle Such a Situation?

- The training officer should understand that they do not know everything and therefore should not get angry with such students. Instead, the training officer should reason and ask them to be more respectful during classes. Some will change, and those who will insist on the same behavior. As a result, the training officer should emphasize those who change for the better and ignore those who resist change because it is something the officer has no power over.

- The training officer should know the difference between pride and ego. The training officer should put pride in the training programs but not have an ego when someone else suggests a change in the program. In many cases, it is advisable to remain humble because training officers are role models to students. The more modest they are, the higher the chances of students copying the same behavior.

- The training officer should also be inclusive of expert opinion. Training officers should be open to the idea that there are people with better knowledge and skills in each area, making them better individuals to address the specific topic or discipline.

In this case, a good training officer should be able to remove their self-interests and ego, meaning that the training officer should go and work well with others to ensure effectiveness and proficiency in the department's training program. My experience as a training officer in handling egos is that it is best to accept that there are people with better certifications and more knowledge than me. As a result, I do not feel low when someone else offers a better idea because I know I may not have all the answers. Allowing myself to maintain an open mind to the suggestions of others helps the team grow stronger, and us deliver a well-rounded and more diversified training program. Training officers should also understand though it may take a career's length to gain buy-in and trust, it also takes seconds to lose the faith of firefighters, making it essential to be cautious in how they behave and act during training.

Buy-In

Buy-in is a critical challenge for training officers because they should win the trust and confidence of the firefighters in training. If more firefighters see the training as boring, there is a higher likelihood that they may not report to it. When they report for training, they may not be as effective as one would expect them to be. As a result, training officers should be good cheerleaders, insisting to firefighters that the training will be good and that they will have fun. A depiction of such a situation allows more firefighters to join in and be more serious with their training. With more firefighters joining the training, training officers should understand that not everybody will support them. Some people will refuse to be part of the training, making it crucial that the officer does not waste time convincing these people to change their ways.

> *"Never Invest 100% Effort into a 10% Problem."*

If 90% of the firefighters participate actively in training, the training officer should focus on bringing the best out of these individuals. The training officer should not waste time focusing their efforts on the remaining 10% who choose not to be bought in such circumstances. Metaphorically, you can hand some people a $20 bill and they'll complain it was folded the wrong way. It should be noted that no matter how much you try to get those people on board with what your vision is of your training program, you may still be met with resistance and negativity. It is easy to fall victim to that mentality, a good training officer should have the wherewithal to navigate past such attitudes and bring forward a good training program that the 90% deserve and want.

These are just a few challenges you will face throughout your journey as a training officer. As these situations arise, as they sometimes will, look back at some suggestions on how to deal with them before reacting. This action will show discipline in yourself and prevent you from losing your following. As we continue into the next chapter, we will discuss two more challenges you will face, personally and professionally, like tunnel vision and ego. Let us continue this journey together as we discuss those two threats and work on a better handling approach.

A VIEW FROM EXPERIENCE

By: Tom Merrill,
Fire Commissioner Snyder (NY) Fire Department

Tom Merrill is a 40-year fire department veteran serving with the Snyder (NY) Fire Department. He served 26 years as a department officer including 15 years in the chief officer ranks. He was chief of department from 2007-2012 & currently serves as a Fire Commissioner for the Snyder Fire District.

Training the Volunteer Fire Department

I have written 35 or so parts to my series of articles for Fire Engineering focusing on the Professional Volunteer Fire Department. The article that generated the most feedback, the most emails and phone calls were an article focusing on training. And most of the comments to me were negative comments, focusing on their department's poor training program or lack of a training program altogether, or worse, lack of any training requirements in the volunteer firehouse. Another common practice in the volunteer firehouse that can be detrimental if not handled correctly is to reduce training requirements as the member gains tenure. Obviously, there are more things to train a new member on, but unused skills can fade quickly so it's important that even senior members still train on a regular basis.

Another potential problem occurs when members choose to hand pick the "easy" drills such avoid the more rigorous or intense drills. So, volunteer firefighters should recognize how important training is and, even if they are seasoned, they continue to train not only to maintain their own personal proficiency but for the overall benefit of the team too. The volunteer fire department leadership should also recognize how important training is, and work to ensure it is a priority focus in their organization. They ensure adequate resources are provided in support of it and they mandate minimum training requirements that are practical and applicable to all members regardless of rank, tenure, or status.

Time constraints continue to be a major obstacle preventing members from getting to drill. There are a lot of other things occupying our member's time. Work and family commitments for sure, but also other firehouse responsibilities. There are often fundraising activities, community events, and other duties associated with a member's elected or appointed position that consume a volunteer's time. Heck, they may be on the softball or bowling team and that takes up another one of their free nights. The fact is, they may find it difficult to arrange to get to that training drill. But I say again, training drills need to be a priority and a professional grade, quality-training program needs to be put together. A professional training program needs to be organized, regular, pertinent, and embraced by every single member.

Organized

The training drill needs to be well organized, ready to go on schedule and leave members feeling like their time was well spent. In many cases, department members come to drill after working a full day at their paycheck-earning job. They rush home from work, maybe have time to eat a quick dinner with the family and rush through homework with their kids (if they even have the time) and then rush off to the firehouse. Or they are giving up a Saturday or Sunday morning to spend time drilling and they may have even paid for childcare in order to go to the drill. If members are taking the time to attend drill, leaders need to take the time to prepare the drills.

Regular

All fire departments should ensure training occurs regularly. And all firefighters should ensure they are regular participants in their departments' training drills. Yes, there are a lot of other moving parts with volunteer fire departments, but training needs to be focused on continuously. It cannot be hit or miss. It needs to be consistent. Members cannot and should not fall back on the excuse that because they are volunteers, they don't have the time to drill regularly. Or worse, cannot expect or hold their members accountable for attending drill sessions.

At the minimum, the volunteer department should offer weekly training drills. Drills should be arranged to also account for shift workers or other members who cannot always make the evening drill.

Pertinent

It's easy to get distracted and focus on other things. Fires could be down as they are in many areas of the country and medical calls certainly make up a large majority of most departments' responses, but a critical element is still fighting fire. You cannot spend close to three-quarters of a million dollars on a pumper (engine) and give it second thought. Even if fires are supposedly "down," they still are the largest cause of property loss in the United States. Even in departments that are slow, remember, the longer it has been since your last fire, the closest you are to your next fire.

Often the little things that add up and cause deaths and injuries on the fireground and so often at what's considered the bread-and-butter type of fire too. But it's also important to take into consideration trains what the community features. Maybe it's residential dwellings. Or perhaps it's a vacation destination (lucky you) featuring an abundance of high-rise hotels. Perhaps it's wild land or agricultural type facilities. Whatever it is, training drills need to focus on what is pertinent in your area.

Embraced by All

As mentioned earlier, it needs to be tempered by all the other demands placed on volunteer's available time. There is no denying the fact that volunteers most precious commodity is time and between working their paid job, perhaps raising a family and any number of other things they could be involved in, there may be little time available to respond to emergency calls, let alone go to the firehouse for that training drill. It becomes a real problem when members prefer to focus on all the reasons volunteers cannot be expected to train on a regular basis.

Instead of thinking creatively and striving to make training a priority, they fall back on the excuse, "We are only volunteers." But folks, we need to remember that we are volunteering for a very serious business and lost in the weekly softball or bowling game and lost in the day-to-day routine mundane calls and business that goes into running every volunteer fire department, is the fact that it is a very serious, dangerous business.

In my experience if training is focused on from the moment a member joins, it is an understood expectation. If well tenured, senior members speak positively about training it also helps motivate newer and less tenured members. Conversely, if they speak negatively, or ignore training, that can also have bad ripple effect down the chain.

I also believe that officers need to participate in the drill – too often in volunteer ranks officers who are not leading the training, often sit back and feel that they do not have to do the training tasks. I believe that those officers should be considered students and should also go through the evolutions. Now, don't embarrass them or yell at them when doing this the first time – talk to them ahead of time and establish that expectation.

I am often asked how to motivate members to attend training drills and improve attendance, and my answers are:

1. Ensure training drills are well organized, planned out and ready to go on time. If members feel their time is being wasted, they will find other things to do on training night (or training day).
2. Train for proficiency, not to fill hours.
3. There is nothing wrong with planning a drill (or drills) months ahead of time.
4. I always liked to have two officers work on a drill together – preferably a captain with a lieutenant. It did two things. The captain could mentor and teach the lieutenant proper drill prep methods. And, if one of them got stuck at work, had a family responsibility or any other last-minute obstacle that can happen in our volunteer world, it ensured one other officer is familiar with the drill and ready to roll with it.
5. Treat members kindly and with respect. Do not embarrass members, belittle members, or harass members. When members needing additional help are identified, work with them on the side in a more private setting if possible. Do not embarrass them or make them feel any less valuable member of the team.

6. Design drills that incorporate all tenures and titles. Have things for senior members to do so they are not sitting around doing nothing and remember to also pay attention to the newest members too as they can easily get lost in the mix.
7. Work hard to get senior members to buy in for attending drills. Maybe use them to help teach or to take newer members aside and work with them. Just a note here that if going to do that, notify the senior members ahead of time so they are prepared and ready. They may want to do some brushing up.
8. Have fun – training should be fun!
9. If possible, have a sit-down meal or some sit down time after the drill to get the members together to laugh, have fun and hang out together. If there is a good mix of membership, this helps eliminate cliques and forms the bonds of camaraderie and inspires teamwork.
10. Over time, other members will hear about how well drills have been going, and hopefully begin showing up – if not, at least new members joining will see how well things are run and continue to come back for more. Hopefully, they also had the expectation explained to them that they need to always attend drills.
11. This is not always easy and may require some effort, but the results will pay off.

A couple of other things: Get members to understand that not everything is on YouTube and available online and there is incredible merit and benefits for members to get out of their own bubble and attend local, regional, and even national conferences. Along with learning, they can benefit from the networking opportunities, which are so important. If possible, get officers subscriptions to Fire Engineering or Firehouse – or other publications and encourage them to constantly stay in touch with what is happening in the fire service.

Spend time teaching officers how to present a drill. You cannot expect a brand-new officer to know how to do it right away but often in the volunteer ranks a member is appointed (or often elected) into the officer ranks, and the expectation is they will be able to prepare and put on a drill right away. This is a major challenge but can be solved by assigning a senior office with them – but should ensure they communicate and work together. Plus, I liked to tell new officers to watch what the good drill instructors do and try and emulate that (from how they are prepared to how they talk to people and how they interact with people and how they lecture a group).

Training During the Pandemic

Obviously, it was a tough time. But rather than simply taking a vacation and ignoring training altogether, the right thing to do was become creative and think outside the box. For us, it amounted to simply getting a Zoom account and charging the officers with putting together Zoom drills – did several during the months we could not get together. It solidified the expectation and understanding that drills are vitally important and even during a pandemic, fires and emergencies still occurred and we had to be sharp.

So, our weekly drills occurred via Zoom. Provided at least an opportunity to review many different things. We also encouraged members to participate in any webinars and training sessions, listen to podcasts and do other things that at least provided learning opportunities.

At one conference I was presenting at, an attendee told me they assigned members to go to the firehouse at different times and different days (spread out over the week) and tasked them with donning and doffing gear and SCBA, going through compartments on the rigs, starting saws (if trained to that level) and many other things to keep them familiar with some of the basics. I thought that was a neat idea.

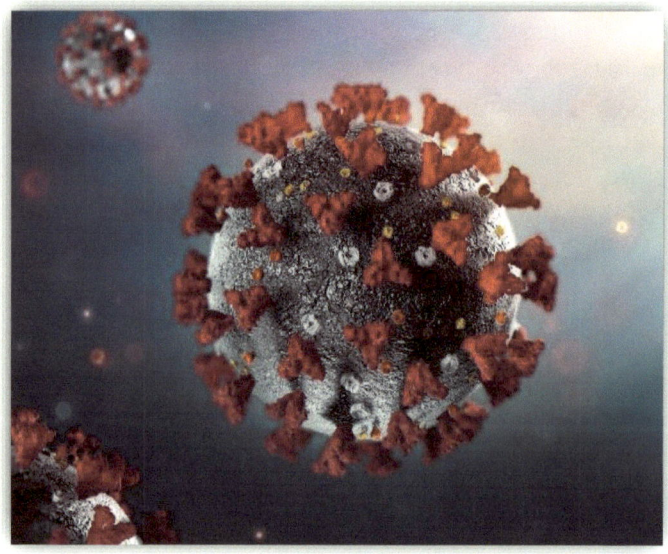

Just like a virus we need to adapt

Chapter 4

Tunnel Vision and Ego

Tunnel Vision

Tunnel vision is a behavior that incorporates a closed mindset, complacency, zero holistic views, and a perception that things should go your way when handling a given action.

Tunnel vision is typical behavior in the fire department. In my experience as a training officer, I have witnessed many firefighters with this behavior, making it challenging to teach them. On the other hand, there are also a lot of training officers who exemplify this behavior, resulting in learning difficulties and low morale.

At first, it may seem harmless, but the behavior's consistency may result in becoming detrimental to the learning environment and the readiness of the firefighters. The risk attached to tunnel vision is great, and individuals not ready to remove this behavior prevents growth to the fire department as well as poses a risk to the well-being of the team and the safety of the civilians. Their reluctance may lead to significant damage to the fire department's reputation. People look to us to provide community safety; if we are too close-minded to integrate new ideas and innovations, we become a danger to our customer (society). Yes, fire departments can be a liability to people's safety. Failing to incorporate the proper measures during training can harm the overall progress of a firefighter's training. Training officers should make it a priority to remove any tunnel vision to allow them to issue the best training to the firefighters.

Having tunnel vision is the same as if you were to tape a rectangular box to your face. What can you see, moreover, what are you missing?

Close-Minded

Having tunnel vision is the same as being close-minded. Close-minded thinking involves refusing to listen to other people's opinions and perceptions because you think you are always right. It is a poor way of thinking because it limits one's development of ideas. A close-minded training officer will refuse any new ideas on training because they think they have it all figured out. As a result, their training ideas become outdated, leading to inefficiencies that may become exposed during an emergency response. Some training officers refuse to update their training methods because of tunnel vision even after seeing that they are out-of-date. Their constant ability to decline to incorporate new and fresh ideas into their training may jeopardize the safety of the community and the firefighters.

Some people may think that a close-minded approach only affects a training officer. This issue is also common among firefighters who think they know it all. These firefighters will refuse to listen to the training officer because they feel their way is better. For example, a firefighter may see their way of handling a specific drill as more effective than the training officer's. As a result, they stick with their idea because they think they know best. In such a situation, the firefighter has a closed mindset, which may jeopardize the lives of others in the field.

How can a Training Officer Handle this Issue?

Be a student of the craft. Training officers should understand that they are students of the craft. This definition means they will never stop learning because learning is a continuous process. Having such a mindset ensures that they do not have a closed attitude allowing them to incorporate new and updated training methodologies.

Moreover, it makes them role models to the firefighters because by continuing to attend training and develop as a training officer will prove to the firefighters that you aren't just pointing a finger and saying, "go do this!" and simply dictating training. This not only keeps the training officer fresh and up to date but assists in them gaining the respect of those they are responsible for. In the long term, the fire department's overall behavior complies with its goals and objectives of ensuring community safety.

Firm but Fair

The training officer should be strict to ensure they get rid of any potential bad apples before they infect others. They should warn such students, and if their behavior persists, they should remove them from their classes. It may sound like a dramatic measure to take, but it is essential if the fire department should continue with its activities effectively and efficiently.

Showing compassion and offering the opportunity at reform is also something that a good training officer should do. If a firefighter shows remorse for their distraction or insubordination, they may be given a second chance. By allowing a second chance after making the "bad apples" aware of what will not be tolerated, helps continue in their development. After all, you are not there to discard people, but to develop them into becoming better firefighters and better servants to the public.

Approach Things from Their Perception

We examined how a closed mindset harms the training officer and the firefighters. This section will identify how a training officer should also approach things from their firefighter's perception. A training officer who is set in their ways and follows through with that methodology regardless of the consequences may certainly put the lives of the firefighters and the public at risk. They believe their method is suitable, making them unable to handle reason and logic.

Practical Situation

A training officer hates simulated training (such as covered face pieces to simulate low visibility training) because they find it unrealistic. As a result, they always ignore simulated training and have the firefighters train on more realistic drills. One of the firefighters tries to convince them that simulated training may benefit them because it will improve their confidence and decision-making in a more controlled environment. The training officer laughs at the firefighter's opinion and tells them to stick to the direction they have been using. They tell the firefighter that their way is better and is what will save them in the field.

In such a situation, is the training officer right to refuse the firefighter's opinion?

1. Yes
2. No

It should be easily understood that in this situation the answer is 2. The training officer is wrong to refuse the suggestion provided by the firefighter. It would be different if the training officer refused to use the simulated training because they wanted them to experience real-life situations to help them feel how that felt in the field. In this case, the objective is to help the firefighters gain confidence during a "walk phase" training methodology prior to introducing them into a more practical setting. Instead, the training officer lets their own tunnel vision cloud their judgement and just throws them into it, which may jeopardize the firefighter's confidence and skillset in the field.

It would be better if the training officer listened to the firefighter's idea, and instead of rubbing it off, they should have tried to see things from the firefighter's perspective and be more welcoming to their concept. On the flip side, the situation would be completely different if the training officer included simulated training but refused to include it in one training session due to a specific need for a practical focus on other essential skills. These skills may consist of communication and judgement calls during emergencies. Firefighting is also about making the right call and not only about one specific task level practical skill. If all training is done with one methodology, this could prevent the necessary level of preparedness for the firefighters while operating on an emergency in the field. Some firefighters may refuse to operate differently because they have only been trained one way.

It is unhealthy for the fire department because making the right decisions during emergencies requires training. Failing to train this ability compromises good leadership in the field, resulting in community risk and threatens injury or worse to the firefighters. In such situations, the training officers are not to blame for the poor perception; instead, their firefighters are to blame. Just because they believe that firefighting is only about getting "salty" and who gets on scene first. This thought process does not make it right to assume essential tasks and proper situational deviation as being applied during an emergency. They should remove their tunnel vision and learn that all training dictated by the training officer can be vital for them.

Complacency Kills

A training officer with tunnel vision is complacent to their training which inevitably will lead to failure, disaster, or death. Complacency makes the training officer lazy to implement better training strategies. Firefighting is an ever-evolving business which requires the training officer to regularly update their training to be up to par with the mandated standards. Failing to incorporate the proper measures to staying current while offering the mission needed training that is both practical and imperative to the development of your fighters can be catastrophic.

Practical Situation

A training officer has significant experience in firefighting, making them develop a predominantly operational training program. They decide to only target the same specific practical skills weekly, and those skills are the only training they require. Even though there are many disciplines that firefighters need trained on to include leadership as one example. This would suggest that a discipline such as leadership training should also be cover throughout the year in the training program. Because that discipline does not favor the training officer's regular training, they refuse to acknowledge it and stick to their own desired method of training.

In such a situation, the training officer allows complacency to affect their judgement by refusing to uphold other disciplines such as leadership training. As a result, the firefighters may be unprepared when it comes to needing to implement leadership skills during emergencies. This can also prevent and possibly regress firefighters who aspire to be promoted in the future due to the lack of the needed leadership training being offered. Due to the training officer's complacency and refusal to be open-minded, they will produce firefighters who only know one way of operating in one specific skill, and therefore incapable of properly performing any other skills that will be needed throughout the duration of their tenure as firefighters.

This can also pose a threat to unprepared leaders operating inefficiently due to their lack of this specific discipline needed in their development through training. This inadequate performance may result in the injury or death of civilians and/or firefighters.

A complacent training officer is worse than a complacent firefighter. Their behavior may affect other firefighters' morale, making them become complacent, and creating an environment of 'status-quo" and downright laziness. A good training officer should establish an environment that encourages a positive flow of ideas and is filled with progressive productivity. The training officer should be ready to deal with such firefighters or students in their classrooms that display this type of negative and complacent attitude in an effort to prevent good firefighters from becoming a detriment, because of the destructive influence that type of attitude can have.

Zero Holistic View

A person who has a zero holistic view fails to know what is within their surroundings. As a result, they fail to identify a problem, making them fall victim to the issue. This is a common scenario in today's society.

Practical Situation

Imagine walking through New York City which is the most populated city in the United States (US) with your nose buried in your cell phone. A person who is walking in this city with all their attention on the phone is completely unaware of their surroundings. Being as they refuse to look up and look around at their surroundings because they're consumed with whatever nonsense they are looking at on social media. In such a populous city, one would be right to conclude the worst for this individual because the individual is unaware of their surroundings.

It is inevitable that one of the possible scenarios that could happen to the individual include:

- The individual may bump into the wrong person and, in some cases, may get "lumped up" and receive a significant beating because not everybody has similar humane levels.
- A vehicle may hit the individual because all their attention is on their cellphone, making them unaware of their surroundings.
- The individual may trip and fall, resulting in physical injuries.

These scenarios are avoidable if the individual decides to be aware of their surroundings instead of their phone. Just like this individual, many training officers are victims of failing to employ a holistic view. A holistic view allows training officers to know what to do in training. By observing firefighters' behavior, the training officer can know when to and what to train on for proficiency in their program.

If the training officer decides to have zero holistic views, the chances of the firefighters suffering from fatigue are high because the training officer is unaware of their current state. In all fire departments, safety is a requirement; that is why the training officer ensures that everybody is undertaking training correctly. If there is one person who is not doing their training correctly, they risk jeopardizing the entire crew's safety in the field. This situation is why there is a need to employ a holistic view.

Practical Situation II

When a training officer is overseeing a structural drill, they should consider the following elements:

- The Rapid Intervention Team (RIT) should be assigned and be equipped with the proper tools. The teams should grab the proper tools.
- All other crews should stage in the right location, and practice good apparatus positioning.
- All crews are performing the assigned tasks they are to be evaluated on during the drill.
- That there is no freelancing going on.

In many instances, the training officer will fail to acknowledge these things resulting in training inefficiencies. Zero holistic thinking makes them unable to see what is happening in their surroundings, limiting their ability to provide the correct judgement. As a result, the firefighters may collect the wrong working equipment, rendering them inadequate for the training.

Another example of things missed could be that the apparatus was poorly positioned resulting in the engine driver leaving no room for the ladder truck etc. Or worse yet a group of firefighters were freelancing, but the training officer failed to notice it and address it either in the moment or during the after-action review. This situation is unhealthy for the fire department because it breeds bad habits by the firefighters thus resulting in bad performance out on an emergency.

Summary

We now know that tunnel vision involves four key elements:

- Closed mindset
- Unrealistic perception
- Complacency
- Zero holistic view

With these critical elements, all remaining is to answer the question, what is tunnel vision? The correct answer should include these four elements.

How to Handle Tunnel Vision

Be Aware of Your Surroundings

One issue with tunnel vision when it comes to training officers is a limited awareness of their surroundings. This problem is why training becomes inefficient because the training officer is unaware of what the organizational need is for both the firefighters and the tactical skillset. By being aware, the training officer can expose any potential gaps or performance weaknesses in firefighters and develop a method to help them overcome their weaknesses. For example, some firefighters may be more proficient in structural drills than others. The fact that there are firefighters who are not at the same level does not mean that the training officer is poor at their job; instead, there may be a need for a more detailed or remedial approach to instruction. One way of remedying the situation is by allowing the proficient ones to train others because they interact with those members of their crew on a daily basis.

There may be something that the training officer is missing out on that a firefighter on the crew may have a better understanding of. Admitting this issue does not make the training officer unable to handle their duties; instead, it shows their ability to empower others by entrusting them with the tasks to deliver the needed methodology in training those other firefighters. If the training officer were unaware of the situation, they would refuse to allow those members to offer the style of training that may be needed. As a result, those who are not proficient in structural drills will not get the training they deserve. In such a situation, the training officer is to blame because they either ignored what the firefighters require in training or were too close-minded to allow other crew members to train others.

Employing a Bird's Eye View Approach

This approach is similar to a holistic view, meaning that one sees things from all angles. It is a typical behavior exhibited by incident commanders. Whenever they investigate an incident, they typically will conduct a 360 and then provide their analysis based on all angles. Implementing a holistic view ensures zero bias when providing an analysis. After compiling a report, they offer it to others for them to see things as how they happened.

This approach is what training officers need. They should employ the bird's eye view in training to determine whether things are going well or bad. For example, this view will enable them to determine whether the students have the correct equipment for a structural drill, that the apparatus is positioned properly, and if they are performing efficiently and correctly. This approach also ensures that the fire department does not waste time and resources.

Giving a Bird's eye view allows us to see the big picture.

Imagine a situation where the engine was forced to position in an area that later turns out that they are too far away from the location of the fire during a drill. The engine will have to reposition to another area to perform the drill effectively. This movement from one location to another wastes time and will reduce the members' attention to training. As a result, the training will be ineffective on that day, and therefore the main objective of the exercise will no longer be the focus. Instead, proper apparatus positioning will be, leading to limiting what the firefighters learned, thus shifting the focus on one specific objective (in this case apparatus positioning) and not on the other objectives that the training officer set in place for the drill. The situation could have been avoidable if the training officer employed a holistic view since they would see a problem with the site before the engine set up on those grounds. Therefore, the training would happen as scheduled, limiting any time wasted, or diversion of learning objectives.

In a case as mentioned earlier, the training officer should set the time aside to ensure this is used as a learning opportunity and that everyone sees and understands the value of proper apparatus positioning. However, nonetheless this needs to be a coordinated and scheduled effort, problems like this that arise during drills that were not meant to include such objectives prove a lack of organization on the training officer's part. This is a situation that should have and could have been practiced prior to the drill.

This is an example of understanding the importance of building your training program with a crawl, walk, run methodology. Proper apparatus positioning should have been instructed and exercised through the driver training program. The fact that the training officer did not deploy the birds-eye view and prepare their people for the proper apparatus positioning forced the training officer to change the drill to focusing on something completely separate from the initial objective. This is just one example of the things that can throw off your schedule and your program without having eyes on things and being organized. I share this specific example as through my own vulnerability, this is an example of my own failure in preparation. So therefore, from one training officer to another…be better!

Ego

In my experience as a training officer, one common phrase is, "we've always done it that way". The phrase is common among training officers and firefighters, making it challenging to impose any new training ideas and philosophies. The phrase originates from ego. Ego makes people reluctant to try things differently because they believe their way is better. It is unethical behavior that may jeopardize the department's efficiency because it means that people will not comply with any updates mandated by the regulatory bodies. They will see them as a challenge, and instead of embracing them, they will refute them because they fail to meet their standards.

Egoism is a character that fosters complacency, an outcome that leads to disaster and death. If the training officer is complacent because of his egoism, a similar nature may develop in the firefighters, making them unable to appreciate any updates on training. The training officer represents what to expect from firefighters; if they have an ego, the firefighters may depict the same behavior. As a result, the organization will nurture firefighters who prioritize their self-interests, a situation untenable for public safety. In emergencies, the risk of causing harm is higher, which may lead to the death of civilians or firefighters. Therefore, if your training program is outdated and complacent because of the "we've always done it that way" mentality, then if someone gets hurt in the field, you should take a hard look in the mirror, you might discover some responsibility caused by self-ignorance.

What Ego Entails

Below are just a few examples of what entails a training officer with and ego:

Unaware of Their Surroundings

Just like tunnel vision, a self-centered person is unaware of their surroundings. Their unawareness is because they think they know better and have nothing else to learn. It is a behavior common in arrogant training officers and "know it all students". These people destroy the fire department's positive culture because they will never accept corrections and always see themselves as a solution rather than a problem.

Arrogant Training Officers

Some training officers are too arrogant to accept their mistakes, making them fall victim to egoism. They see a correction as a challenge to their authority, a concept they believe no one should try on them. In reality, it shows a poor leader who is ready to make others feel inferior because they are insecure about their authority. The situation only indicates egoism as an unhealthy character to have by leaders. I am not saying that you should see yourself as a problem but as a student of the craft. Having this humble mindset will enable you to know that you will not always be right and that regardless of your certifications, there is someone who knows better than you. This mindset will inform you of your surroundings because of your eagerness to learn. The reverse is what is evident in many fire departments.

The "Know It All' Students

The "know it all" students are the type of people who are unaware of their surroundings. They believe they know everything and that their way is more justifiable than the training officers. These students continually ask questions only as a tactic to trip up the training officer to prove that they know better than them. As a result, they create a destructive environment for learning because their behavior might affect those eager to learn from the training officer. It is unfortunate, but one which training officers find themselves in during training. These students see themselves as the potential for the future, indicating their inability to grasp what their environment entails.

Because they do not see themselves as potential a distraction to others, it indicates how little they know of their environment. The resulting situation is a toxic environment, making it difficult for any learning to happen. Dealing with these types of people can be a challenge. Some suggested tactics to use could be but not limited to the following:

- Engage with the individual and have them help build the training program.
- Explain how their interruptions are distracting others.
- Attempt to encourage them to use their knowledge and experience as a positive influence on others.
- However, it should be noted that a last resort may be eliminating the bad apples before making the entire class rot. It is a decision that you may use if you are keen on demanding respect.

Egoism leads to one being close-minded because they see their ideas as better. They become immune to reason, a behavior that limits their learning potential. This behavior is a direct insult of the methodology that training officers are students of the craft. This behavior ensures that officers are not learning. Inadequate learning can be through refusing to listen to the updates instructed by regulatory bodies or refuting any ideas suggested by the students.

Dealing with egos is like carrying unneeded extra weight, you won't get anywhere.

A training officer with this type of behavior becomes unapproachable and firefighters fear approaching them with their issues because they do not know how they will react. As a result, it limits training effectiveness because students will do it to finish rather than understand them. Close-minded officers also foster a hostile environment because they nurture the same behavior in the students. In the previous chapters, we highlighted the role of a training officer as that of a role model. A close-minded officer will breed the same behavior in firefighters, leading to a situation where firefighters become reluctant to change. They see their ideas as the only solution and do not face any challenges, resulting in possible issues in the field.

Working with other departments will be difficult because they want their approach to be applicable and not others. They often use the phrase, "we always do it that way," because they want others to use their way. Such a culture will build a poor image for the fire department, and it will be a matter of time before a catastrophic event happens. This situation may include the death of a firefighter or a civilian.

Ways Training Officers Can Avoid Ego

Be More Approachable

As a training officer, you should be more welcoming to others. The more people feel open around you, the easier it is to eradicate egoism. A fire department is like a family, which requires all people to be present for it to be more effective. An approachable training officer becomes aware of the firefighter's struggles and limitations because the firefighters will tell them. As a result, the officer dictates a schedule that will fit their firefighters. For example, if a firefighter has anxiety and stress, putting such a person in the field would be inhumane. Their risk of making poor decisions is high, making it crucial that the training officer puts them on desk duty.

In other cases, it would be advisable for them to take a leave.

Such an outcome can only happen if the training officer is aware of their surroundings. Their understanding improves if they become more approachable.

I know you are asking yourself how a training officer can be more approachable. It is straightforward. Try the following steps:

- Be more empathetic
- Ask the firefighters how they are handling different life aspects
- Be open-minded when dealing with them
- Instead of focusing more on the cause of a problem, focus more on its solution

With these four steps, a training officer will become more approachable, making them eradicate egoism. As a result, instead of insisting on the statement, we have always done it that way", they will focus on the statement, "what can we do to make things better". As little as it may sound, the message will ensure that training officers quickly reduce egoism and that firefighters relate to them.

Test Your Understanding

A training officer gets feedback from the firefighters about his training. The firefighters believe that the structural drills are ineffective and requested that the officer find other ways of training the drills. The officer immediately tears the paper and calls for a meeting. He says that the training is practical if they put their dedication to it and stop whining. The training officer believes he is doing the right thing by demanding that the firefighters work hard instead of complaining.

1. Is the training officer right?
   - Yes
   - No
2. Do the firefighters make a compelling case, or are they whining to get out of a tough training?
3. If you believe the firefighters have a compelling case, what can the training officer do to ensure that the firefighters relate to his training?

Staying Current

A training officer should incorporate newer training ideas to get the best out of the students. Firefighting is an evolving process requiring those in control to comply more with the changes to ensure the best learning environment. In my experience as a training officer, I learned that training officers will always be students of the craft. As a result, it makes sense to ensure that all training methods are up-to-date and comply with the guidelines stipulated by the regulatory bodies.

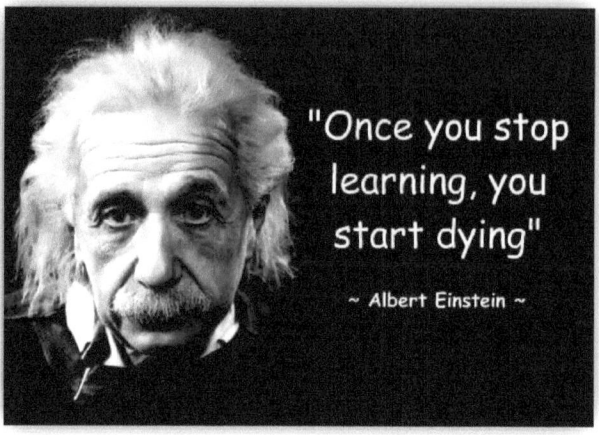

Be a student of the craft, never stop learning!

It is not the training officer's duty to refuse to teach the new training ideas; instead, it is their duty to filter and know what to teach and ignore until they master the basic training. Such a mindset allows them to be more proactive in handling training instead of having a closed attitude about the training changes.

Test Your Understanding

As a training officer, you receive new annual requirements regarding training. There is an increase in the number of training classes, and this situation is unfavorable for you. You decide to ignore the changes and stick with the previous requirements.

1. Is your decision appropriate?
    - Yes
    - No
2. What decision was the training officer supposed to take?
    - Ignore the changes
    - Integrate the changes into training
    - Filter the changes and decide on which changes are appropriate

Relevant

A training officer should ensure that the training is valuable and practical. For example, when a training officer teaches firefighters how to react to an emergency, their reaction levels increase because they know what to do. This situation is evident in how firefighters handle their field jobs. If there are zero efficiencies, coordination, and cooperation, there is a likelihood that their training is ineffective. In such cases, the training officer is to blame because the training he offers is irrelevant.

You may be asking yourself how a training officer can offer relevant training. The training officer can fulfill this action through:

- Ensuring that they maintain an open mindset regarding different ideas and innovations
- Reading various materials about training to remain updated with what good training entails
- Foster a training program that sustains your mission needs.

These three procedures will ensure firefighters receive better training, evident in how they deal with their jobs. They will have better knowledge and expertise in handling emergencies, allowing them to provide life safety.

In short, I hope that some of the items covered throughout this chapter have either opened your eyes to some of your own short-comings, or that they have developed an awareness so that you can learn how to properly deal with these things as they arise. As we continue, we will learn about organizational and cultural dynamics.

A VIEW FROM EXPERIENCE

By: Mike Scotto,
Lieutenant (ret.) Fire Department of New York (FDNY)

LT Scotto has been in the fire service since 1979, and recently retired as a Lieutenant with the FDNY in Nov. 2021. He has multiple experiences during his tenure with the FDNY from Engine 18 in Manhattan, TL. 157 in Brooklyn, TL. 58 in the Bronx. Instructor at Randall's Island "the rock," Instructor with the Rope Unit. National Fire Instructor Level 1 & 2. New York State (NYS) Fire Instructor, Orange County (NY) Fire Instructor, Master Exercise Practitioner (MEP) certified through Homeland Security. 9/11 and the "Valentino Fire" Brooklyn 1996 survivor. Instructor at FDIC, NYS Fire Chief's Conference and other venues throughout the US. Featured on podcasts "Networking for Success", Getting Salty #85, FDNY Fire Pro.

The role of a training officer in a fire department is crucial for its success. While some may perceive this officer as a "buff," which signifies a deep devotion to the fire service, their primary focus should be on addressing both obvious and subtle needs within the department. Even if the training officer doesn't have an enthusiast label, they must possess a strong desire to ensure that all members have a comprehensive understanding of firefighting.

One key responsibility of the training officer is to proactively anticipate and address future training issues. This includes continually updating and maintaining the department's training policies, which should encompass a wide range of topics such as Fire Engineering, ventilation tactics, Hurst tool operations, and line placement. Additionally, they must stay vigilant regarding changes in equipment, construction features, tactics, policies, personnel, and technology that may affect firefighting operations. This necessitates extensive research, often involving late nights or early mornings.

The training officer understands that ignorance is not an excuse in firefighting, and they are committed to preparing their members thoroughly. Much like a cook who meticulously prepares a meal, the training officer ensures that all the necessary elements for training are in place. Just as a cook ensures the spices are ready, the meat is marinated, and the oven is at the right temperature, the training officer ensures that members are equipped with the knowledge and skills they need.

The training officer also plays a critical role in maintaining the relevance and currency of academy training. This involves regular evaluations to identify and address any deficiencies in candidates early on. By doing so, potential issues can be resolved before they become significant problems, minimizing the chances of failure in real-life firefighting situations.

Once new members graduate to the firehouse, the training officer's responsibilities shift towards making them feel welcomed and part of the team. It's important to instill a sense of pride and belonging in new members, emphasizing that they are part of the best company in the department. This sense of identity and belonging is fostered by both the unit's officers and senior members, with the training officer serving as a critical role model.

Leadership within the fire department is essential, and the training officer is often at the forefront, guiding the way. Much like a ship at sea, the fire service faces numerous challenges, but with a clear purpose and strong leadership, it can move forward successfully. In the fire service, unlike some other fields, there are no refreshers once a firefighter is officially in, which places the responsibility on the training officer to ensure ongoing training remains a priority.

Coordination among officers is another key role of the training officer. They should not seek "yes-men" but experienced officers who are dedicated to maintaining their companies' readiness. Occasionally, training may be seen as an inconvenience due to other events or priorities, and in such cases, the training officer may need to adapt and compromise to ensure training continues effectively.

In some instances, senior members may lose interest in training, leading to bad habits. To prevent this, senior members should take the initiative to lead training exercises in the firehouse, setting a positive example for younger members who are the future of the department. Informal reviews of operations can also be beneficial, allowing members to openly discuss what transpired and learn from each other's experiences.

As training progresses, it's essential to acknowledge that members learn at different paces. Training should not be perceived as a punishment, and one way to keep members engaged is to let them choose training topics that interest them. This approach empowers members to take ownership of their training, ensuring their active participation.

Ultimately, the success of the training officer lies in their ability to bring together individuals with diverse experiences and backgrounds to function as a cohesive unit. This ongoing effort, like preparing a delicious meal, requires dedication, adaptability, and a commitment to the department's mission. The well-prepared firefighter is the ultimate goal, and the training officer plays an important role in achieving that success.

Chapter 5

Organizational and Cultural Dynamics

In many fire departments, new training officers are guilty of ignoring the present culture and ruling with an iron fist. Many firefighters fail to respond to this situation because there is zero mutual trust. Without mutual trust, the likelihood of injuries during drills is higher because firefighters may be reluctant to do what their training officer says. As a result, it becomes essential for the training officer to provide a foundation where the firefighters trust them, allowing them to follow instructions naturally.

Despite this situation offering the best results, many training officers ignore the humanistic culture and follow their beliefs in creating a new culture. In some cases, it may work, but it fails to bear fruit in many situations. Humans will always resist what they do not know, especially if there is minimal persuasion to do an action. As a result, the fire department risks becoming a massive calamity with zero order and instruction.

Avoiding this situation requires the training officer to adhere to six steps of improving culture through training. These steps include:

- **Prepare**
- **Communicate**
- **Encourage**
- **Motivate**
- **Value the Culture**
- **Mutual Trust**

Understand that the application of these steps is important. However, much like a strategic plan, there will be moments when these steps overlap or when it becomes necessary to revisit a previous step. Throughout the cultural improvement process, continuously refer to and reassess these six steps, ensuring they are effectively guiding your journey.

Prepare

Webster's Dictionary defines the word prepare as a verb, meaning to *make (someone) ready or able to deal with something*. This is important to understand because this should be the first action you take in how you are going to help improve your organization's culture. Ben Franklin was quoted *"By failing to prepare, you are preparing to fail."* If you do not take the time to prepare your team for the proposed vision you have for the training program, you will inevitably be setting yourself up for failure. This failure will be caused by the lack of reception and unwillingness to buy-in to what that vision might be. Therefore, it is extremely important to prepare your team for what is to come.

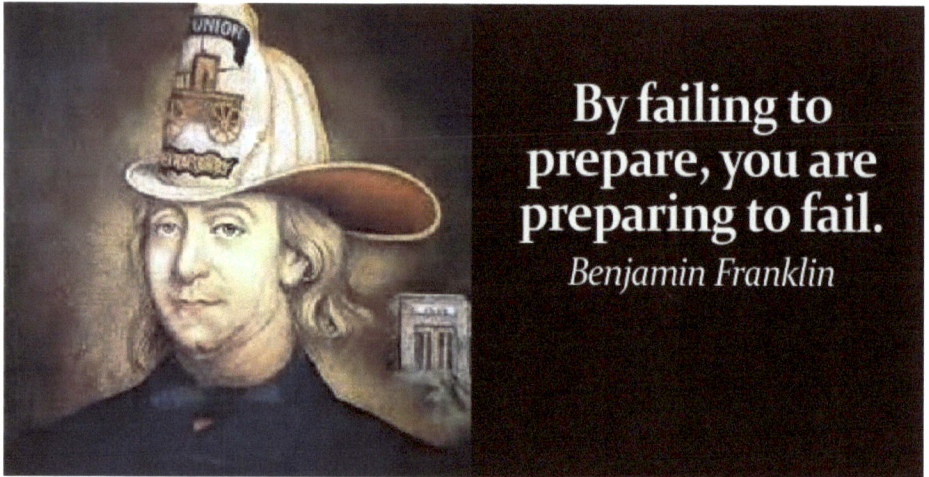

Ben Franklin sums up the importance of being prepared.

This step involves preparing the team for the new change. In many situations, firefighters have a standard training program they believe to be correct. This situation makes it essential for the training officer to prepare them for what is to come. Good preparation involves the training officer hosting meetings with them and encouraging them that they can do better. These two steps ensure firefighters understand what is to come and what the training officer expects. As a result, they will know how to react to the new training. The reaction can include raising their frustrations and informing the training officer of what they think the training should entail.

Hosting Meetings

You probably have attended meetings at one point in your life. Most meetings have an agenda where the chair communicates with the members about the issue. The chair expects to understand the current situation and listen to what the members say. This situation applies to the fire department.

If you are a training officer in a department, it is important that your team is in line with your vision. This is a situation that may seem difficult for a new training officer. In certain cases, the new training officer's credibility may be in question, or firefighters may be leery of the training officer's intentions which makes the firefighters seemingly unwilling to embrace the training. Therefore, hosting meetings with each of the members of your team is important. By hosting meetings, the training officer can get to know their people better. They can get an understanding of the culture of the department and the current pulse of the training program. This situation will help with gaining the buy-in that the training officer needs from the firefighters and ensure that they face minimal resistance. However, it is important to understand that through these meetings, one should be genuine and not say what others want to hear. There may be times in the future where what you said can come back and haunt you. Stay away from making false promises to gain a following, it never lasts. Instead, treat these meetings as if you do when running command.

Start with meetings if you are a training officer struggling to implement new training in your department. Consider a meeting in the fire department like any other ordinary meeting and let everyone have their say on the issue.

Other concerns to ensure are:

- Be more of a listener at first to ensure that you collect information from the firefighters.
- Provide a comfortable environment in which firefighters will feel free to say what they are thinking.
- Be considerate of their issues to let them know that you understand their frustrations and issues.

Encouraging Them to Do Better

When holding these meetings, the sole purpose will be to encourage them to accomplish better things with training. You should think of this process as a situation where you are selling a product, and in this case that product is you and your training program. The more convincing you are at showing your team that they should buy this product, the easier it will be to gain their following or buy-in. This situation applies to this phase. A training officer should convince firefighters to allow their firefighter to follow them. It is important to note however, you can lose that following in an instant! Effort should be made daily on maintaining their support and buy-in.

A non-convincing training officer will face significant scrutiny and prejudice because firefighters will assume they know better. I know you are asking yourself what you can do to ensure you are more convincing.

It is simple. As a training officer, you should include the following elements to sound more convincing:

- Talk with firmness, ensuring that you do not intimidate the firefighters.
- Refer to your experience in the field to earn their trust and respect.
- Be more empathetic.
- Listen to their ideas.
- Do not let them coerce you into aggreging with their ideas because it may come out as weak.

These steps show what a training officer should do to ensure they offer the best encouragement to firefighters. You should remember to make them come out naturally so that the firefighters feel they are talking to a person, not a robot. As a firefighter, you should expect to experience different issues in these meetings. Firefighters will raise their frustrations about various things, and as a training officer, you should respond to their problems with empathy, fairness, and authority.

Communicate

I know you have heard this phrase countless times. It is a simple action that many people ignore, costing them their ability to be better leaders. **A training officer is a leader**, making them a vital person to incorporate this philosophy. A training officer can use and apply communication in different ways.

Informing

A training officer should ensure that they do not have any secrets. Secrets ensure that firefighters feel left out of training, which introduces resistance. The training officer should inform the firefighters of the expectations and their different training roles. For example, if a training officer is unhappy with how the firefighters handle the technical rescue roles, they should inform them and tell them what changes they want. The earlier the firefighters know these changes, the easier it becomes to prepare for the change. In many cases, minimal preparation is what leads to change resistance.

Open Dialogue

An open dialogue is when both parties have the liberty to talk. One-sided communication leads to bias and poor results because people are afraid to share their opinions. Without opinions from both parties, it becomes challenging to determine whether the information is appropriate for both parties.

Training Deficiencies

A training officer can communicate to the firefighters about their weaknesses. For example, firefighters skilled in rope rescue will be poor in engine company operations. This situation makes it critical for the officer to address how to handle this situation. The officer can prioritize their strengths, ensuring they improve on their strengths. On the other hand, the officer may prioritize their weaknesses and ensure they work to improve on them. Regardless, the situation ensures that the officer manages the firefighters' deficiencies correctly to ensure they do not become a liability to the team.

Hard Conversations

These are conversations that the training officer may need to have from time to time. The training officer should be able to deliver hard news when firefighters are not meeting the program's expectations. As a result. However, a good training officer should not judge them; instead, they should encourage them. Training officers who react this way often end up shutting down their firefighter's motivation and passion, which causes the firefighters to react negatively to such situations. It is wrong because it shows the officer is not empathetic to listen to what the firefighters expect.

These conversations may be unpleasant, especially if firefighters need to work harder to achieve a given milestone. For example, if the fire department is experiencing a budget cut, the situation may lead to inadequate props. As a result, you may be put in a situation where you need the firefighters to assist with building training props that are needed to ensure they receive the best training. Making these props may demand a significant amount of extra time dedicated by the firefighters.

Their reactions to the situation may be because they feel they are being worked or over-tasked. The budget cuts alone may weigh heavily on the workforce's morale and then have an impact on productivity. Due to the nature of them having to build their own training props, not only proves their perceptions correct about the budget situation, but also leaves the training officer open to comments like "this isn't my job" to impact the culture throughout the organization. Being empathetic by listening to them and sharing their pain may be a turning point for them to put their issues aside and work to improve their training. The situation goes back to what we discussed in the first step, being a good listener.

Test Your Understanding

A training officer holds a meeting with the firefighters to illustrate his ideas on new training. They indicate that all firefighters should listen to what they say and not share their frustrations. Furthermore, they note that the training will include additional hours working on their rope rescue drills. The officer states the action will improve their ability to be better in field rescues, which clearly, they lack because of their current training.

Despite the officer's good intentions, they refuse to listen to the firefighters' opinions and views on the training. What is the likelihood of the firefighters' listening to the training officers' philosophy on training in the long term?

The firefighters may refuse to listen to the officer long-term, especially if they maintain the same attitude. At first, they may incorporate the new ideas indicated by the officer, but with time, they may fall out with him. Firefighters are like any other humans. The more unnecessary force one applies on them, the more the urge to resist, especially in critical matters. As a training officer, you should learn the value of maintaining good listening skills and having open dialogue to allow each to share their opinions on various topics.

Vision and Plan

Communication allows the training officer to issue their vision and plan. For example, the officer may state the new training is mainly to improve their attention in drills to ensure they do not lose focus in the field. The vision may be to ensure that firefighters are not at risk of getting hurt in the field or worse. Such a vision and plan allow the firefighters to commit to the plan because they know it targets them positively. A vision and plan that does not target the firefighters' needs may be challenging to implement because of the resistance it may face.

Encourage

Encouragement allows the firefighters to understand they are part of the organization and have a considerable investment in the project. The training officer should ensure that firefighters share this belief to increase participation.

Good Treatment

The training officer should talk to them like stakeholders. A stakeholder is someone who has a considerable interest in a company. Their interest may be financial or emotional. Stakeholders include consumers, shareholders, and employees. In a fire department context, stakeholders are firefighters, the public, and any authorities having jurisdiction over the fire department.

If the training officer frames things to their firefighters that they may have something to lose if they do not commit to the project entirely. This situation can make them eager to perform because they want to be part of the training.

Encourage Participation

Participation ensures task completion. Without it, training cannot happen. The training officer should ensure that firefighters share the same spirit of participation. For example, if a firefighter is more skilled in technical rescue or rope rescue, the officer can put them in charge of training in that activity. On the other hand, if a firefighter is more skilled in engine company operations, the officer can put them in charge of developing a program to minimize any deficiencies.

This role allocation allows the firefighters to participate actively in the training because they feel like they have something to lose if they do not. It is a good way of managing firefighters, especially those with an ego.

Motivate

As a training officer, you should understand the benefits of motivation. Motivation improves work performance and builds trust. These two components are essential in any workplace because they ensure long-term survival. Motivating firefighters may be a tedious step, especially if a training officer is a dictator and one who believes that their way is always right. The situation makes it impossible to listen to reason, resulting in conflicts.

If you are a training officer seeking to motivate firefighters but unaware of where to start, follow these procedures. The procedures include:

- Motivate individually or in small groups
- Focus on the benefits and not the negatives
- Understand motivation frequencies

Span of Control: Motivate Those that You Influence.

As we learned through the span of control, an incident commander should only have control of 5-7 people. The same methodology should be used when recruiting and attempting to influence others. Focus on the 5-7 people who you know are bought into your vision. Inspire them to take that vision and inspire the 5-7 people they have influence on and over time the program will become a success. Meetings ensure that each firefighter raises their opinion about the suggested training, allowing the training officer to react to their issues. The officer can instruct them on why they think the training is appropriate for them. The more meetings they have, the higher the likelihood of gaining their trust. Firefighters feel part of the change process instead of having a dictator who believes their opinion is correct and everybody should follow. A training officer should avoid attempting to motivate firefighters in large groups. Large groups have different personalities, including those who want to resist change and those who want change. In some situations, negative characters may overpower those willing to incorporate change, wasting time and resources.

Test Your Understanding

A training officer calls a meeting of all firefighters to discuss the need for the firefighters to help with the construction of the training props. The training officer understands that due to budget cuts the department is unable to purchase materials or have contractors work to build these props. As a result, the firefighters now have to make their own props. The training officer believes that encouraging the group as a whole will save time and make the prop construction easier. Is it an ideal situation for the training officer?

- Yes
- No

The answer is no. A larger group may increase the possibility of having a bad influence on those who may have been bought in if briefed in a smaller group. Some firefighters may be willing to help but unfortunately may be influenced into refusing by negative firefighters who were present during the briefing to a larger group. As a result, it can create a toxic environment between those who may be ready to help and those who don't. The training officer should have considered using the "span of control" methodology to motivate those who they have the most influence on. Let's say hypothetically, if they were to motivate a group of 5 firefighters to draft a plan on how the training prop construction should be laid out, they could work on that plan as the small group of 5 and then take it to those that they each have an influence on.

Because of the nature of span of control, each of those 5 firefighters also has their own level of influence on 5-7 people. By doing this in a smaller setting, the process will allow more opportunity for firefighters to be "bought-in" on the training prop work and less resistive.

Focus on the Benefits and Not the Negatives

As a training officer you should celebrate your team's wins. For example, if you have a "green" firefighter who has struggled in their tactical performance over the past, but recently displayed a great deal of improvement at the most recent training event, you should celebrate their improvements. This not only will encourage others to continue to work towards improvement, but it also proves the progressive nature of your training program, through the growth of the proficiency in operational skillsets of your firefighters.

On the other hand, if the training officer chocks up this recent improvement as mediocre and dismisses the positive development in that firefighter, that training officer may be perceived as a person who does not validate the work of their people, which can result in a regression of skills caused by an unwillingness to train hard.

Understand Motivation Frequencies

Motivation is vital, but it may be detrimental if used poorly. Too much motivation nurtures robots and not firefighters. A training officer should understand when to use motivation, ignore it, and use other measures. In some cases, too much motivation may lead to complacency. Training officers should use more motivation during the early phases of change and slowly reduce it to allow firefighters to have a personal obligation to work. The training officer can incorporate motivation if they feel the firefighters desperately need it. Understanding this frequency leads to better training performance because each individual will understand their role.

Value the Culture

Culture is what people in a specified community believe to be correct. This situation makes it challenging to come and change their culture because it may lead to resistance. The situation is similar to a fire department. Firefighters have a culture where they do things because they believe it is correct. As a new training officer, you cannot demand personnel change immediately because human nature will resist. It requires time and convincing in order to allow them to leave their old standards for the new.

Test Your Understanding

Fire department *XYZ* has firefighters who understand their training starts in the morning and takes three hours. They have two drills they perform, including the rope rescue and engine company operations. Their previous training officer told them to focus on these drills to better their field performance. Their training officer resigns, and you become the new training officer. On arrival, you indicate that their training sucks and should change immediately. You refuse to listen to why they do things that way and insist that your way is better.

What is the probability of the firefighters resisting the philosophy implemented by the new training officer?

- Very High
- Very Low
- Not a chance

The answer is very high. This situation is because the training officer is reluctant to understand how the firefighters performed their previous drills. They are ignorant of the department's culture, which impacts his ability to relate with them. This predicament makes it impossible to maintain a healthy relationship with firefighters. One behavior that you can allocate to this training officer is egoism. Egoism derails the training officer's ability to see things rationally because they believe his way is better than the current. Despite the situation being correct, the officer should be willing to listen and understand why the firefighters value their culture.

Cultural Understanding

Understanding the culture will limit conflict because the training officer will display that they understand the ways and beliefs of the firefighters. As a result, the firefighters will appreciate the intention of the training officer. The situation may bring to light some concepts the training officer was unaware they could integrate into their training. Furthermore, the training officer may know what to relinquish what they see as inappropriate to the new regime. Relinquishing these concepts will be because the training officer would have studied the culture. Where there may be outbursts concerning the situation, the training officer can explain their reasons to make the firefighters understand why they did so.

Understand Why Firefighters Have Pride in Their Actions

An activity that firefighters enjoy doing is one that the training officer should be careful not to destroy. It is important to value and understand that many firefighters take great pride in certain things. Some examples may be but not limited to, their company or station number, their logo, their performance, and believe it or not, the color of their fire trucks! Not joking... Some firefighters take an enormous level of pride in the fact that their fire truck is green, or blue, or yellow, while others (the better firefighters, of course lol) take great pride in the fact that their trucks are red. As the training officer, you should analyze why the firefighters enjoy doing those items so much.

As we've discussed in Chapter 2, you are a leader, so if some of the things that they take pride in are inappropriate, you should be firm and relinquish those activities. However, if you relinquish them, you should be careful not to upset your firefighters but instead, be willing to listen to other solutions they may provide and provide the reasoning behind your need to make a change. As a training officer, your role is to direct and not judge how firefighters perform their duties. The more directive you are, the easier it becomes for firefighters to comply with the directions you want them to uphold.

Mutual Trust

After engaging in the previous steps, establishing mutual trust becomes easy. The firefighters understand why you want to implement a given philosophy and why it is vital, they do it. Training officers should understand that trust does not come naturally and is not something they can force into someone. The earlier you understand this concept, the easier it is to implement a new culture, one that a majority of the team believes in.

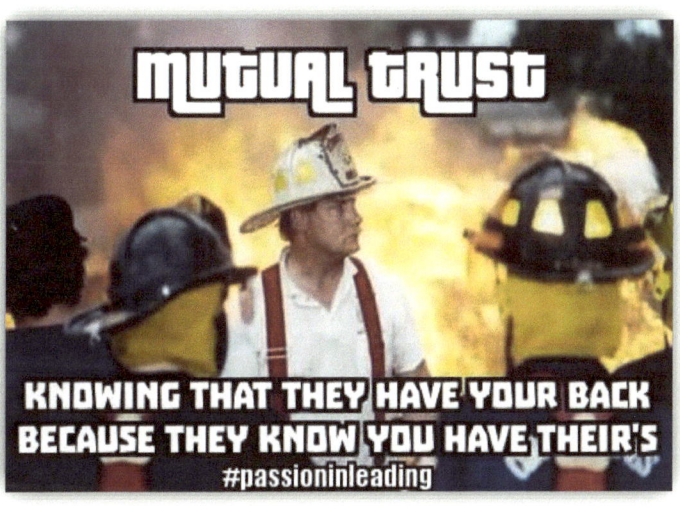

The importance of establishing Mutual Trust

Activities That May Increase Mutual Trust

Elimination of the Fear of the Unknown

The more transparent you are with your firefighters, the easier it is for you to aid them in erasing their fears. In many situations, firefighters fear change because they do not want to do things differently. As the training officer, you should explain the vitalness of incorporating an open-dialogue philosophy and the benefits it has on organizational growth. By doing this, you will increase communication which will remove negative perceptions and help eliminate the fear of the unknown.

Understand that Firefighters Fear What They Do Not Know

In the previous section, we discussed that firefighters would fear what they do not know, resulting in resistance. As the training officer, you should be open to this fact, but leave room for some negativity when implementing this new philosophy. Firefighters are not robots. They are ordinary people and will be reluctant to change if they do not know what the change entails. Training officers should allow firefighters the opportunity to air their frustrations to ensure they formulate ways to combat their situation.

The Importance of Being the Why and not the What

I was recently listening to a presentation given by Simon Sinek; in it he details the value of being the why and not the what. He describes this value by telling a story about the company Apple and their invention of the iPhone. He gives an example by telling a story about when Steve Jobs and his team began constructing the phone, they knew that many consumers knew what a smartphone and a cellphone already were.

Despite this concept, they wanted to make the iPhone a great product in the market because they understood what people wanted. The humanistic concept is what arguably makes the iPhone the more preferred product in the world. The phone is not unique because it is a smartphone like any other phone, but because Steve Jobs understood humanistic concepts, they could market the product to people in a way that made them think the phone was the world's best product.

Simon Sinek describes the importance of being the Why.

This concept is what training officers need to incorporate. They need to sell the why and not the what to the firefighters. The why allows them to be considerate to the firefighters, making them better training officers. As a training officer, you should continuously ask yourself whether you are selling the why or the what to the firefighters.

If all your responses lead to the "what" question, then it is high time to evaluate your training strategies to improve participation. The point here is this, no one cares about what you are, they already know that you are the training officer, firefighters care about why you are their training officer and why you are the person they should trust to develop them and their organization. Training officers should understand that firefighters are not interested in what title or rank it says on your office door or on your email signature, but instead in why they should trust you to be their training officer. The "why" question convinces the firefighters by letting them know that the training officers are more empathetic and have their best interests at heart. The "what" question relates to the training officer's role description, something firefighters already know. Be the why!

Effects of Lacking Mutual Trust

We have explained how to earn mutual trust and the importance of it. We should discuss the negatives of training officers lacking mutual trust with firefighters. This includes injuries during drills and line-of-duty deaths.

Injuries During Drills

Inadequate mutual trust can lead to firefighters questioning your methods during training leading to reluctance. Despite your way being the right way, they refuse to incorporate them because they doubt your ability to teach them. As a result, they get injuries because they did not listen to what you told them.

The training officer is as guilty as the reluctant firefighters because you did not take the initiative to ensure the firefighters trust you. You can earn their trust through team-building exercises. The more exercises you incorporate, the easier it becomes for them to trust you because they understand your philosophy.

Line of Duty Deaths

Firefighting has a higher risk of fatalities, especially if the training is not appropriate for the firefighters. If you fail to incorporate better training without establishing mutual trust, your training will certainly result in deficiencies. If firefighters are reluctant to train with your measures, their chances of performing poorly in the field are very high. As a result, the risk of them getting hurt and the community safety being at risk is very high.

Test Your Understanding

An incident commander assigns a neighboring mutual aid department to the Charlie side of a structure to throw ground ladders. However, the mutual aid officer did not trust the incident commander's instructions and decided to ignore them. As a result, there are no ladders thrown on that side. Later, a firefighter operating interior was met with unsafe conditions, which forced that firefighter to bail out of the second-floor window on the Charlie side. The department is liable for negligence.

Who is to blame for this situation?

- The incident commander
- The officer
- Both

The answer is Both. The mutual aid officer is liable for negligence because they refused to listen to instructions provided by the incident commander. Moreover, the incident commander is also responsible for the situation because they did not establish an environment for the officer to trust them. Because both parties lacked the needed trust for one another's competence to properly execute the assignment left a side of the building unladdered, thus creating a vulnerability with the crews operating inside.

This situation is a practical illustration of the importance of having mutual trust. As a Training Officer you should understand that mutual trust is essential in the fire department; without it, people may reject the instructions provided by those in authority.

My Experience as a Training Officer

I have worked for a department which was experiencing budget cuts, which yielded a situation where the department was seven firefighters short. The shortage of personnel leads to training complexities. For example, there was a training session with six firefighters who had previously completed the training. It would be inappropriate to ask the six firefighters to participate in the drill again and could result in them losing their drive to continue to give 100% effort during training evolutions. This made it difficult to stick to the training schedule as well as made it impossible to keep people engaged due to feeling overworked from being stuck at the firehouse for 3-4 days only with a 24-hour break in between shifts.

Furthermore, there were shortages in props because of the budget cuts. We could not get the Department of Public Works to finish the props, leading to a situation where I had to ask the team to help build the props needed to finish the training building. It was something I had to do because there was no other option. Because I knew I was asking a lot from the team, I did not force them into doing the action but asked them while framing it in a way that gave them the sense of ownership and buy-in due to them truly building the props. By doing this, they embraced the task and are proud of the fruit of their labor because it is truly their training building. The activity served as a team-building exercise, which indicated the purpose of mutual trust between the training officer and the firefighters.

In the next chapter we will discuss the importance of mutual trust and some tips on how the training officer can secure mutual trust with their people.

A collapsible floor is a great example of practical training props constructed out of donated wood.

A VIEW FROM EXPERIENCE

By: Steve Prziborowski,
Deputy Chief (ret.) Santa Clara County (CA) Fire Department

Steve Prziborowski has over 30 years of fire service experience, recently retiring as a Deputy Chief with the Santa Clara County (CA) Fire Department. He is an adjunct instructor for the Chabot College (CA) Fire Technology Program and is still actively involved in the fire service through speaking, writing, coaching, and mentoring personnel aspiring to either get hired or get promoted. He has authored and published four career development books: *"Reach for the Firefighter Badge," "The Future Firefighter's Preparation Guide," "How to Excel at Fire Department Promotional Exams,"* and most recently, *"101 Tips to Ace Your Promotional Exam,"* and "Courage Under Fire Leadership," a topic he passionately speaks and writes about to ensure today's leaders are prepared for tomorrow's challenges. For more information or to contact him, please visit his website at www.code3firetraining.com

The Company Officer as the Training Officer

As a fire officer (company officer responsible for their crew and/or firehouse, or a battalion chief/shift commander responsible for multiple crews and firehouses), I believe your primary duty and responsibility is training and mentoring your personnel.

One of our former fire chiefs used to ask aspiring or newly promoted company officers what they felt was their most important duty and responsibility. The most common answers were along the lines of what I expected: to ensure the safety of my crew and that they go home safely to their families; to take care of them (meaning the community who is allowing us to be in the unique position to help them in their time of need – regardless of whether we are career or volunteer); to handle things at the lowest level; to solve problems; to do the right thing; etc. Very few usually mention training and mentoring their personnel.

Now before you tune me out because you are one of those believers that we are here for them (we are, I'll get to that) and that's all that matters, or that we need to be safer and do a better job of not getting killed or injured (we should, I'll get to that as well), and/or you think I'm downplaying serving the community and taking care of our personnel, hear me out and I'll show how both of those beliefs tie into training and mentoring our personnel.

Many fire officers are quick to say that training and mentoring may not be their primary duty because they have a department training officer and/or training division whose main focus should be training and mentoring. I used to be one of those as a newly promoted company officers years ago until a wise battalion chief tuned me up saying something to the effect of: "our training division has 3 people for 300 personnel. There is no way they can ensure you and your crew are trained in everything and to handle anything. That's your job as the company officer, so make it happen!" Now I wasn't that naïve to fail to realize I did have a duty and responsibility to train myself and my crew, not to mention mentor them as I knew I did (it was in the job description for company officer that I did actually read before getting promoted), but my complaining that day to my battalion chief basically blaming our training division for not giving us all the latest and greatest, most relevant training, was something many are guilty of even today – being a recliner sniper, or just someone who wants to point fingers, blame others, complain about things and point out problems (most of the time without solutions or at least reasonable, realistic and/or sustainable solutions).

So how does training and mentoring tie into ensuring we are doing our best for them and doing our best to try to reduce firefighter injuries and/or line-of-duty-deaths that may be avoidable (some are avoidable, some are not based on the risks we many times need to be taking for the right reasons)? Let me explain.

By taking ownership and knowing the importance of training and mentoring our personnel as officers, we have a better chance ensuring the following occurs:

- Our crew is prepared for their current and future positions, even if they have no desire to be promoted. Not everyone is meant to promote or should promote. Some are meant to stay at their current rank and there is nothing wrong with that. But regardless of whether someone wants to promote or stay at the same rank, it's critical to ensure that they are up-to-date with best practices, that they are trained and prepared to do their job and do it darn well, and that they are never retired in place and calling it in every day by being a slot filler.

- Our crew knows the strengths and weaknesses of our team collectively and individually. Why? Because our mission is accomplished through teamwork, whether it is a team of two on a minor emergency response or more than twenty on a working structure fire. As an officer, if you don't know the strengths and weaknesses of your team, and as anyone on the team, if you don't know the strengths and weaknesses of your team, there is a great chance you won't use your team to its fullest potential and you may be wasting opportunities to capitalize on certain strengths or talents, and you may be using certain people in the wrong capacity, such as in an area they may not be strong at, which might lead to a delay or accomplishing the mission we are tasked with.

- Our crew actually gets the job done and done right. Our crew is ready to handle "it". What does it mean? Anything we may find ourselves being challenged with on any given day that ends in "y."

- Our crew is taking care of them by doing the previously mentioned items effectively, efficiently, appropriately, timely and for the right reasons.
- That we are not relying on our training officer and/or training division to prepare us for ANY situation as they cannot. If you've never done time as a training officer or in the training division, you may not realize this, but they don't have the time or resources to ensure we are all trained for anything and everything, as much as they would like to.

Think about it: upon getting hired, you probably had to already be trained or your department trained you to the firefighter 1 and/or 2 level to allow you to function at the basic beginner level on a fire company.

While your training division may schedule daily, monthly or annual training for your crew, they are going to first focus on what is known as the mandatory training, the items that are required by the Occupational Health and Safety Administration (OSHA) or other state or federal codes, by your state or local emergency medical services agency (for those that are EMT or paramedics) related to annual recertification requirements, or what may be best practices as determined by the National Fire Protection Association (NFPA) or the Insurance Services Office (ISO).

Regarding NFPA, while I say best practices, there is no "NFPA police." Also, most departments don't actually adopt NFPA standards (as they would then be on the hook for actually following them which can always be a challenge for a variety of reasons, two being staffing and money), the various NFPA standards could still be held against our actions or non-actions should something significantly tragic occur and it was determined we didn't follow or attempt to follow NFPA standards because we felt we had a better way of doing things or didn't feel they were important.

Regarding ISO ratings and best practices, for those states and departments that may be on the hook to go through the grading process, where a higher ISO score might lead to reduced insurance rates for the community, then those best practices that account for points when being graded (such as number of training hours in certain subjects, individual and company training hours, building familiarization and pre-fire planning, annual and refresher certification training for various ranks or positions, etc.) would probably be pushed out as required training to the members.

The main reason the training division will usually provide (push out) this training throughout the year is because in all honesty, we can't expect each fire officer to remember what is mandatory or not mandatory as well as how many hours are required. And even if they did know the difference, if you really look at a lot of the mandated or best practice training (such as bloodborne pathogens or legal things such as supervisor harassment training), very few fire officers would prioritize those topics that aren't as fun or exciting as the hands-on stuff outside of the classroom and in the field.

When I served as our training officer, I reminded the crews and fire officers that the main job of the training division is to provide the recruit training for new personnel in the form of an academy, and then provide the mandatory training to ensure the highest priority mandated items were accomplished, to help reduce liability to the department. It was up to the fire officer to ensure they and their personnel were trained at the individual, company, and multi-company level for whatever it was they may be faced with. Yes, as the training division, we would try to keep them up-to-date with best training practices and to also try and have fun training when we can (fun usually meant hands-on, pulling hose, flowing water, throwing ladders, etc.), but that the fire officer needed to know the strengths and weaknesses, not to mention individual and company needs at their level. We were a resource as the training division, but we couldn't be at all 15 of our firehouses and with all three shifts of personnel as much as we would love to, especially when there are over 300 personnel now being served by a staff of six in the training division.

Our crew is up-to-date with what is going on in their department and in the fire service. Knowledge is power, and information is out there if you go look for it, ensuring you have vetted out the information and are not providing inaccurate, incomplete, or inappropriate information, which is worse than providing nothing. If you are not subscribing to publications such as Fire Engineering or Firehouse, and then sharing the relevant and timely articles with your crew, you're missing out on them gaining valuable information that may better prepare them to do their jobs. If you are not staying abreast of key email lists that send out relevant and timely information such as from www.firefighterclosecalls.com or www.dailydispatch.com and then sharing them with your crew, you are doing them a disservice and ultimately your community a disservice. If you're not attending training events and conferences locally, at your state level or at the national level (such as FDIC or Firehouse Expo), you're missing out on valuable information to pass along to your crew. If you're not encouraging them to go with you, you're missing out on them experiencing some of the best training and mentoring, not to mention networking that is occurring.

I challenge you to never get in the rut of thinking, "I'm just a fire officer." If that's the case, it's time to retire and pass the baton to one of those you've hopefully trained and mentored over the years and is willing to do your job, do it right, and take it to the next level. As a fire officer, I get nobody ever wants to have a firefighter die or get injured on their watch. But on the opposite end, as a fire officer, nobody should ever want a civilian to die or get injured on their watch. When they could have made a difference by being more aggressive and taking necessary risks when the situation dictates.

It can be a fine line at times trying to balance the needs of your personnel and the community, but we can never forget why we are fortunate to be here – for them. And them is not just the community, but our personnel. If we don't ensure our personnel are trained and mentored to be the best they can be, how can we expect them to be delivering their "A game" when the bell goes off and someone is having their worst day and something we can do might make the difference in their life, their health, and/or their property.

Train and mentor others like your life, their lives, and the lives of the community depend on it – because it matters!

Chapter 6

Coaching, Mentoring, and Mutual Trust

As a training officer, these three elements are things that you should incorporate daily in the fire department. These elements ensure that everybody understands their role and works towards improving the department's performance in ensuring community safety. Many times, I witness people confused between coaching and mentoring. They may be coaching but call it mentoring and vice versa. All training officers should understand coaching and mentoring to ensure they realize their full benefits. These two elements require mutual trust between the firefighter and the training officer. Recognizing the positive impact of coaching and mentoring becomes challenging if there is zero mutual trust.

You may think that you are a good coach or mentor, but firefighters do not trust you because they think you do not have their back. As I often say, mutual trust is "knowing that they have your back because they know you have theirs", I say this because that simply exemplifies what mutual trust entails. If you, as a training officer, do not support or have your firefighters back when needed, they will not have yours when you need them. As a result, it becomes difficult for them to sacrifice their time for you because they know you will not do the same for them.

In the previous chapter, I mentioned how my firefighters sacrificed their time to help me build training props while we were facing funding limitations. Without mutual trust, I wouldn't have been able to get the "buy-in" to get them to help me because it is not a task that they are typically responsible for. They could have resisted and filed a grievance to delay the development of the training grounds, being as it was more of a contractor, or Department of Public Works (DPW) skill and responsibility. As a training officer, when reading this chapter, ask yourself if your firefighters trust you and if you trust them.

Coaching

Let us get into it. What is coaching? What does coaching entail? Does a training officer need to be an excellent coach to be successful?

The answers to all these questions will be covered in this chapter.

What is Coaching?

Coaching is a method of **directing**, **instructing**, and **training** a person or group to fulfill a goal or specific skills to the assigned group. When coaching someone, the coach may want to ensure the group understands specific skills and uses them to achieve a given milestone. On the other hand, they may want to ensure the group does a particular activity well. This situation is similar to firefighters. A training officer who is also a coach should ensure they spark the untapped potential of their firefighters to improve their performance.

You may have realized that I intentionally stated the training officer should recognize the untapped potential of the firefighter. This situation is because coaching does not make a training officer introduce new talents to the firefighter. The firefighter should have the spark within them to allow the coach to fire it. Without the desire from the firefighter, a training officer cannot be an excellent coach to them. As a result, a training officer can be a good coach if the firefighter is a good student.

As Bob Nelson said, "you get the best efforts of others not by lighting a fire beneath them but by building a fire within them". The quote illustrates the significance of someone having the desire to complete a task for him- or herself rather than waiting for someone else to complete it for them.

What Makes a Good Coach?

A good coach should have the following characteristics:

- They should create a suitable environment for others.
- They should have mutual trust.
- They should be keen on the three elements: direct, train, and achieve skills.

A Good Environment

A good environment involves the following factors:

- Not being a dictator
- Good development
- Paint a picture that they have the correct tools

Not Being a Dictator

A good coach is not a dictator. A dictator believes that only their way is right, and everyone should comply with their regulations. If you are a training officer, you should not have such behavior because it disqualifies you from being a good coach. As a good coach, you should ensure that firefighters are open to tabling their issues and discussing them with you. If firefighters cannot discuss their problems with you, that means the environment is inconducive for them, which is a failure from you as a training officer.

A training officer is responsible for creating a good environment. If the environment is hostile, there is a possibility you are a dictator. A dictatorship environment ensures resistance from the firefighters, leading to poor work performance. Commitment becomes an issue in the workplace, and those that have it slowly lose it because they cannot ensure the dictatorship.

A training officer should avoid such a situation by demanding that all firefighters have equal rights in what they have to propose. The officer should treat every firefighter equally and ensure a democratic environment where every firefighter has a say in what goes on in the department.

A good coach should avoid such a situation by ensuring that the workplace is a comfortable environment that warrants inspiration and offers constant development. As the training officer, anytime that you are instructing a class or leading a drill, the methods that you educate on while "in-the-moment" are coaching. For example, if someone pulls a hose line inefficiently without properly flaking it out, and utilizing proper hose management to ensure they get the most amount of hose deployed. That interaction with them where you make the quick suggested changes to teach them in that moment about why they should've pulled the hose the way you are suggesting… that is coaching! Good training officers have the ability to apply those traits that the workplace is a creative and developmental environment. Where the training officer can offer those quick and in-the-moment nuggets of instruction that help maintain proficiency throughout their people

Good Development

A good coach ensures that they offer the required development to their firefighters. The training officer shapes their talents to match the expectations they demand in training. Moreover, this situation illustrates Bob Nelson's quote I mentioned in the previous section. Good development requires the training officer and the firefighter to offer something to yield results. Coaching becomes obsolete if the training officer or the firefighter is unwilling to tap their potential.

Paint a Picture: Show Them Their True Potential

A good educator motivates their students. Motivation allows them to find their true potential. For example, a training officer should encourage their firefighters to not give up on completing a task. They can encourage their firefighters to find it within themselves to tackle the task no matter how difficult it may seem at first, because they know that their people can do it. As a result, the firefighters work toward achieving the expected goals, creating a better motivated team of firefighters who are more tenacious during training.

People perform at their best when they feel they are trusted. As a result of that, they will then offer their trust back to their superiors. Productivity and the ability to execute tasks at the most efficient level of performance are at an all-time high when there is mutual trust.

> *"Knowing That They Have Your Back,
> Because They Know You Have Theirs."*

This situation also applies to the fire department. A firefighter will commit to a training officer's project if they know the officer has their best intentions at heart. If they witness any reluctance from the officer to have their backs, the firefighters may lose their trust in the officer forever. For example, firefighters can expect that the officer trusts them when they issue new suggestions for training. However, if the firefighters make recommendations that are valid and may improve training, yet their training officer rejects them, it is a situation that may reduce the trust between the firefighters and the training officer. Without mutual trust, how can you expect to get everyone to comply with your directives? You can't, that's how! If you are still unwilling to agree with the impact of mutual trust, look at the situation from another perspective.

Three Elements of Coaching

Coaching incorporates the elements **directing**, **training**, and **instructing** to realize the full potential of those being coached.

Directing

Directing ensures that firefighters perform a task appropriately. For example, if the training officer wants the firefighters to be efficient in engine company operations, they should guide the firefighters in how they want them to do it. Good directing requires good communication that sets regulatory expectations as well as overseeing how firefighters follow instructions.

Training officers are often guilty of not overseeing what they want firefighters to do. An officer may issue a guideline on how they expect the training on engine company operations should happen but fail to be in attendance at the issued training. As a result, the possibility of errors increases, indicating the training officer is a bad coach.

Training

The name, training officer, has the word train in it. Therefore, it indicates that the training officer should be capable of training others because the name has the word, train in it. I know that may seem too simplistic, but it indicates the vitalness of a training officer being able to train their firefighters. Good training involves using the correct equipment, overseeing the whole process, and ensuring that each firefighter improves their performance. The more they improve their performance, the higher the likelihood of the firefighters maintaining a level of proficiency resulting in the training officer being a good training officer and an excellent coach.

Instructing

Instructing involves providing guidelines on how training occurs. Without proper instruction and knowledge in the subject can likely cause confusion in training. Confusion leads to underperformance, a failure of the training officer. A good training officer will guide the firefighters on performing different drills and ensure they stick to the stated philosophies. As a result, the situation indicates the training officer is a good coach.

Mentoring

A mentor is an experienced or trusted advisor, as such they are responsible on advising or training someone. Mentors rely on experience to ensure that their mentees (students) reach their long-term goals. The keyword here is long-term. A mentor focuses on the long-term output of an individual. A training officer should be an excellent mentor to ensure that the fire department's long-term objectives are attainable. One objective can be community safety. The increment of community safety is something that requires long-term analysis. It is impossible to realize community safety immediately because it involves incorporating different strategies that may start to be productive after a while. As a result, it illustrates the training officer's role as a mentor. The officer should include different training strategies to improve training. Better training leads to better performance by the firefighters and community safety.

Mentoring is the Keystone to Success

A keystone is something that holds everything together. It is the strength that improves performance. Before looking at mentoring as the keystone, let us dive into a practical example to help you understand what a keystone is.

Have you ever wondered why Pennsylvania is considered the United States (US) keystone? When the US was fighting for its freedom from England in the late 1700s, Pennsylvania was the center where Virginia and Massachusetts leaders met. At the time, there was no internet and flight transport. People had to use strong horse wagons to meet at a destination. The central point of the meet-up was Pennsylvania because it was at the center. In that state, leaders met and came up with different regulations. The founding documents included the Bill of Rights, the US Constitution, the Declaration of Independence signing, and winning independence from England.

These documents are essential to American history. As a result, Pennsylvania has become the keystone state in the US. Without it, it is likely the US could not be what it is today. This description makes it essential for training officers to understand their role as the keystone of the fire department.

Training Officers as the Keystone to Success

A training officer should be a good mentor. They hold everything together, including the firefighters and the middle and upper management. Without them, there is no connection between these three parties, leading to inefficiency within the department. A training officer who understands this role will likely be more productive in their responsibilities because they will train firefighters to their best capability. The more they train them, the easier it becomes for the upper and lower management to perform their duties. A good mentor advises someone on what to do. To advise someone, you should first listen to what they are saying. A training officer should be a good listener and be supportive when the situation demands it. For example, if a firefighter comes in with an issue, the training officer should be willing to listen and advise them appropriately.

Test Your Understanding

A firefighter came into my office and told me he had to quit. The firefighter was a good person but had issues. He was struggling with substance abuse, specifically alcohol. At first, I knew the firefighter was not cut out for the job, but that was something I did not want to talk about with him. Instead, I listened to the firefighter's complaints and offered him support. I realized that I had to empathize with the firefighter because he struggled with various issues.

Did I perform my duty well?

- Yes
- No

The answer is yes because I listened to the firefighter and supported him. Many times, people want to talk and express their frustrations. It is crucial, especially in the fire department, to listen to these issues because they indicate a firefighter's struggles. It may be their only way of expressing their frustrations about a given subject, allowing them to reduce their stress and anxiety.

Another lesson from the story is about creating a good environment. If I had not created a good environment, the firefighter would be afraid of coming to inform me of his intention to quit. He may have decided to carry on knowing that the job is doing more harm than good to him. The idea that the firefighter was confident and trusted me to tell me of his struggles indicates how vital it is for a training officer to be a trustworthy individual.

The more trustworthy an officer is, the higher the indication the officer is an excellent mentor to the firefighters. Firefighters look to them for direction and leadership because they know they will not lead them astray. These lessons are what all training officers should learn to ensure they issue the best training to firefighters.

Differences Between Coaching and Mentoring

Coaching is a verb and a method of directing, instructing, and training a group or person to achieve a goal. Coaching is dependent on the three elements mentioned. Without them, it is impossible to coach firefighters because there will be zero directives on what is happening. Coaching happens now. It is a short-term "in-the-moment" solution intended to yield success immediately.

Mentoring focuses on the long term because the process is continuous. In a fire department, the long-term goal is to ensure community safety. Achieving this situation demands that there are different strategies available to yield success. The mentor should implement these strategies, and they all focus on the long term. This situation makes mentoring a continuous process, requiring patience and consistency to show success.

What is Involved in Coaching and Mentoring

Availability

A training officer should always be available. Firefighters have different issues, making it essential for the officer to be available. I always ensure that my door is open for those wanting to discuss their problems. In other situations, people may want to talk about issues that are non-related to firefighting, and I choose to listen. I listen because I know how vital it is to create a bond with firefighters. They easily trust me because they know they can share what their frustrations are, and I will not judge them.

Test Your Understanding

A training officer claims he is a good coach and mentor. Many firefighters say that the training officer is rarely available when they want to raise their opinions about various issues. At one point, the training officer comes and calls a meeting and tells them he is trying his best to be there for them, but time is the problem. Is the training officer justified in raising such a response?

- Yes
- No

The answer is no. Before you took the job as the training officer, you understood what the role entails and the sacrifices you had to make. It is okay if the training officer was always available and then his availability was reduced because of a family emergency or another related emergency. In this situation, the training officer is always unavailable. The training officer does not value his role, they created an untenable environment for the firefighters. This situation may lead to reduced work performance which may impact community safety.

Good Listener

A training officer should do more of the listening than the talking. In many situations, the training officer should guide, counsel, and listen to what the firefighters say. Listening enables the officer to evaluate the situation and provide the required response that may positively impact the other party.

I try to make it a priority to hear out the firefighters that I work with, a reason why the couch in my office is never empty. People will always want to come and raise their concerns with me because they know I will listen. For example, even the fire chief will come and sit on the couch in my office and talk to me about the fire department. He will also talk about other issues that do not relate to the department. I listen to these issues because I want to and may learn about things I did not know.

Trustworthy

Trustworthy people will always make other people feel comfortable talking about themselves because they know the person will not misuse the information. They understand that the individual has their best intentions at heart. A training officer should integrate this behavior to become a good coach and mentor.

Do you remember the example of how I showed you how a firefighter of mine told me about their issues and their intention of quitting the fire department? The firefighter could not have told me his intentions if he did not trust me. He trusted that I would not use the information he gave me to undermine him or misuse it. As a result, the firefighter spoke out about his intentions to quit the department. Trust is essential in the fire department. As a training officer, you should ensure your firefighters trust you to make them share their issues with you.

Test Your Understanding

A firefighter is going through anxiety and stress caused by recently getting divorced. Recently, his ex-wife has requested more money towards child support. The firefighter is struggling but is afraid to talk with his leadership because he is afraid that they may use that information to gossip about him and his current situation. As a result, he has been working multiple overtime shifts but stays in his room and is not maintaining his proficiency training. One day while operating the pump during a live fire drill, he failed to put the pump in gear (due to a lack of attention), leading to the hose line not being charged which resulted in significant injuries by one of the firefighters.

Who is to blame for this situation?

- The firefighter
- The training officer
- Both

The correct answer is both. The firefighter knew he was not in the right frame of mind to train but ignored that factor, putting others at risk. The firefighter could have sought help elsewhere or decided to take a temporary leave of absence to improve his mental health. The fact that he chose to continue with training is personal negligence.

The training officer is also to blame because they created an environment where the firefighter thought he could not trust them. The training officer should ensure that they are open to firefighters and that they trust them to share their issues. Failing to do this action is negligence by the training officer.

Supportive

A training officer should be empathetic to firefighters. When firefighters open up about their struggles, the officer should not make fun of them but support them. Supporting them can incorporate different things. For example, firefighters can listen to them and say nothing because some firefighters may only want that outcome. In other situations, the training officer can advise them on tackling their issues.

The officer should know which outcome to incorporate and when to do it. Mentoring and coaching will enable this task by instilling the correct behavior in training officers.

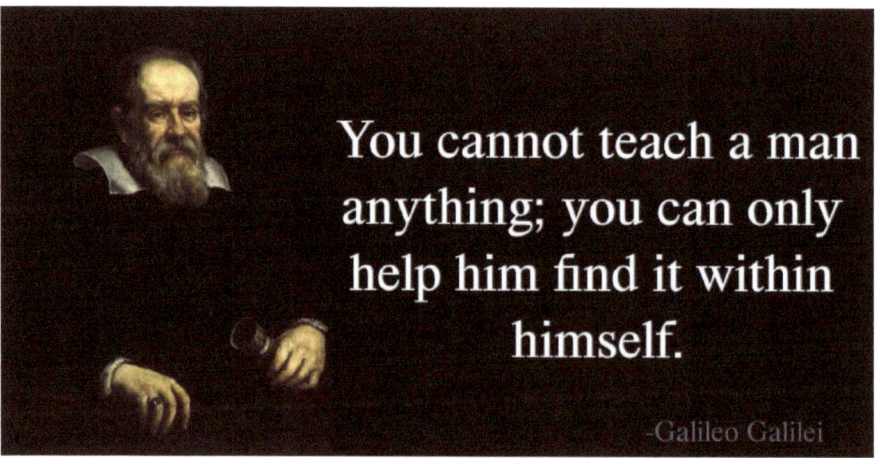

This quote helps illustrate **support**. Galileo exemplifies what being supportive entails. Being supportive to your people should be a high priority trait of a training officer. A supportive training officer will help struggling firefighters rediscover their potential, enabling them to tackle the issue affecting them.

Inspiration

Who is a good coach and mentor? This person encourages others to be better. Human behavior may limit one's potential to encourage others to be better because they are afraid that they may surpass their achievements. This situation should be unavailable to any training officer because it discourages improvement. A training officer should always encourage firefighters to be better than them. Yes, they may achieve better training and certifications than you, but that should not be your focus, instead you should be finding a way to offer them opportunities that were not awarded to you when you were a firefighter. I have a list of items on a dry erase board in my office under the category "To Do" and the second to last objective is "Be the training officer that you wanted when you were them." If they accomplish more than you, it indicates how well you perform

Consistency

Consistency involves ensuring that you apply the same responsibility or action to different people. As a training officer, you should avoid favors because it indicates bias, which may lead to a hostile environment. Human nature will always lead to individuals like one person more than the other. The situation does not mean that you are justified in favoring one person over the other. It only means that you have more things in common with that person than the other.

Test Your Understanding (1)

Imagine a situation where five people are in a room and each given a bottle of water. The instructions are to independently provide feedback on how the water tastes after drinking it. They can also describe the water bottle and what they think about it. The assignment has to include zero discussions.

What format will the participants' answers take?

- They will be very different
- They will be the same

The answer is they will be different. Everyone sees the world differently, so in this case, not every response will link up and may seem very different from one another. In addition, there are to be zero discussions, each participant will provide feedback regarding the issue. There will be concepts they provide that the creator of the activity may not have anticipated. This situation defines why consistency is vital. Each participant has strengths and weaknesses, making it essential that there are no favors in the workplace.

As a training officer, you should maintain consistency in how you deal with your people. The differing views of others in your organization is why your organization is a success and your training program hinges on your ability to tap into those strengths that others may have and build on their weaknesses too.

Test Your Understanding (2)

I worked with a firefighter who contested with me for the training officer position. I got the position but did not have bad blood with the firefighter. The firefighter had a bad attitude, which is why he never got promoted. I knew this situation and aided him with guidance and counseling because I understood his problem was that he never got the required coaching.

Was I right in doing this action?

- Yes
- No

The correct answer is yes. As a training officer, you should not owe anyone favors. Being consistent allows you to treat everyone fairly, encouraging a good workplace environment.

As a training officer you will have to coach your people on a daily basis. Moreover, the very nature of your existence is to mentor them because you are responsible for their future development. Lastly, the training officer serves in the capacity of a counselor and "go-to" person at times. Being that most times the training officer is not in a direct supervisory role, they represent a position that firefighters may come to for advice. That position comes with a huge level of earned responsibility, that responsibility is gained through mutual trust. If your people won't talk to you for anything other than training specific topics, you may want to check on whether or not there is a level of mutual trust with you and your people.

Mutual trust is something that carries over as we expand on our training programs and start to network with people from outside of our agency. As we continue into the next chapter, we will discuss in detail how to build a training network.

A VIEW FROM EXPERIENCE

By: Larry Conley
Deputy Chief, Collinsville (IL) Fire Department

Larry Conley is Deputy Fire Chief of Training with the Collinsville Fire (IL) Department. Conley has over 30 years in the fire service. He has a bachelor's degree in fire administration from Columbia Southern University and is currently pursuing a master's degree in organizational leadership.

Historically, people and fire have remained consistently linked. The fire service profession is unique in its relationship to this link. When fires are out of control, firefighters are expected to use their unique set of skills to mitigate. Fire + person = Firefighter. People also need teachers to provide guidance and training. I'm sure with a bit of research we can find some form of teaching that represents the "training officer" even before it became the position we know today. Teacher + Delivery of Structured Fire Knowledge/Wisdom/Passion = Training Officer. Those who are lucky enough to work in the position of training officer are connected to a principled historic lineage of teachers. This is why the position should be taken seriously.

Most of our successes can be traced to teachers. Great teachers can help us reach our full potential. Even bad teachers can teach us what *not* to do. The training officer is the key to departmental readiness. They help us maintain a balance of efficiency and effectiveness in the delivery of services. To be efficient the TO is expected to keep the department compliant with ISO, OSHA, NFPA, NIOSH standards etc. Effectiveness means the department is trained to deliver world class all hazard mitigation in their communities. When this balance is disturbed, the department and ultimately the citizens suffer. The buck stops with the fire chief, but the training officer bears a great deal of responsibility. At their core, firefighters are committed to laying down their life for strangers. This is the ultimate in service and sacrifice.

The training officer should have that same intensity when it comes to delivering the best training possible. Ideally, their training should reduce injury, loss of life and give firefighters the best chance to save life and property in the community. Training officers, who remain students of their craft, will always have something valuable to teach. Things such as studying books (like this one), attending workshops, utilizing a mentor, obtaining accreditations (like CTO), mastery of core skills, learning new skills, perfecting your instructor/teaching skills, membership in associations (like ISFSI), participating in instructor cadres that do hands on skills regularly, being a contributor to respected forums via podcast, panels, magazine articles, national/local conventions, etc. keeps the TO sharp. It also presents endless opportunities to provide up to date training to your department. The training officer who networks with other training officers and respected sources in the industry will enjoy the benefits of the *Iron Sharpens Iron* principle.

Remember, you as a TO are linked to a proud principled history. Being a great firefighter, teacher, helps you lead and make people better. Apply the correct amount of pressure. Take this calling seriously. Give yourself grace and room for growth. Fire, people, and hazards are things that will never go away. Departments who are masters of mitigation will have the safest communities. The key to a department's readiness is a great training officer.

Chapter 7

Building a Training Network

I inherited a training program that needed fine-tuning, changes, and guidance. The program was not exclusive to everybody, meaning the training did not incorporate every person. It was challenging initially. After all, proper training should also include mutual aid partners because these people will be in the field during emergencies. Imagine a situation where you have never trained with anyone from another fire department, and an emergency comes where you have to work together. It will be a total mess from start to finish. You may pull off a win in the beginning, but it is something that will not last if you do not train together frequently.

After reading this background, ask yourself the following questions:

- Why are you reading this book?
- What are looking to accomplish?
- What needs to be brought to your training program?

These questions will help you evaluate your training program and your performance as a training officer. Throughout this chapter we are going to discuss how networking with others can help strengthen your training program and improve the skillset of your firefighters. Understanding how to network with others and what you can gain by networking will assist you in creating goals for both your team and yourself. Networking with others will help you accomplish those goals while developing partnerships with those around you.

What is Networking?

My personal definition of networking is a meeting of minds gathered together to create greatness. People have different explanations for networking.

I believe networking has the following definitions:

- It is exchanging information and services between individuals, groups, and partners.
- It is the cultivation of productive ideas for organizations.

These explanations have two vital segments: exchanging information and services and cultivating productive ideas. This information exchange is compulsory because there will be different people in the room talking. They may provide different knowledge or information on any upcoming or new standards for fire department training and tactics. As a result, people can generate ideas on how to comply with these standards.

The cultivation of productivity is important in any organization's success. Bottom line, the more you network and share information, the more you will be in the know. The more you are in the know, the better prepared you are to design a training program that practices versatility and remains up to date.

Steve Hamilton's Definition

Steve Hamilton, Captain Fort Jackson (SC) Fire Department, summed up networking by so eloquently describing it as "it all starts with a handshake and a smile." It is that simple. A smile and a handshake may be the two things that save your departments from experiencing the negative impacts of budget cuts and other potential threats that may be facing your organization.

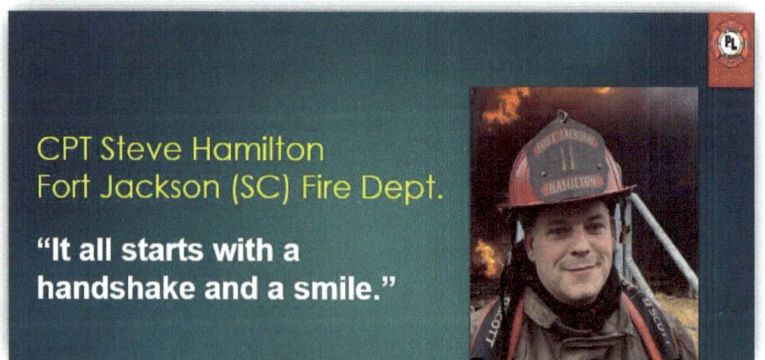

This process can also help you in other ways through networking. One example is people from different fire departments may converge in a room to explain the current issues with new training requirements. They may formulate ways to ensure that most fire departments comply with these requirements to avoid unnecessary setbacks.

Building a Training Network

Franck Ricci's Definition

Frank Ricci, Battalion Chief (ret.) New Haven (CT) Fire Department, defined networking as "removing the awkward divide."

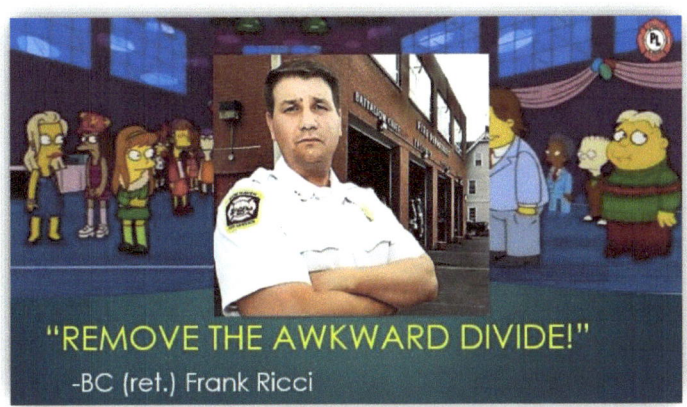

Practical Illustration

Assume you are at a school dance and all the boys are on one side and the girls are all on the other. Neither of them is willing to come out and start dancing with the other because they are shy and in fear of rejection. If no one is brave enough to start dancing with one another, there is basically no point in even having the "dance" because none of them have summoned up the courage to walk across the dance floor and ask the other to dance. The reality is that if one person were to build up the courage to ask another person for a dance, others may be inspired to do so and be courageous to ask for dances as well.

Now imagine this illustration when managing a training program. If you know that there is a resource available (whether neighboring department or business owner) and you are too afraid to reach out and ask them to offer their services that will help strengthen your training program, you're knowingly subjecting your team to the potential of being inadequately trained due to their lack of resources available. All it takes is one person to connect with those neighboring resources. If a person were to reach out and start networking, that awkwardness will eventually fade away. It's easy, remember what Steve Hamilton said, "it all starts with a handshake and a smile." With this notion, there should be no reason for an awkward divide.

What Networking Entails

Four essential steps generate the networking process. They include:

- Marketing your mission
- Building relationships
- Sharing knowledge
- Remaining open-minded

Marketing Your Mission

As you begin to start networking with other organizations, you should go into it with the intent of marketing your mission. While looking to recruit others to join forces with you to help improve the training needs of your team, be sure to be a cheerleader for your organization. Be a champion for your vision and your people. Let others know what types of skills and services your people can offer. For example, if you have a group who has a strong skillet in engine company operations, you should take this as an opportunity to talk your people and their capabilities up. However, don't overdo it, make sure you follow-up your "bragging" session with humility. Express your recognition of certain gaps or weaknesses. That is where you gain ground by building the outside organization up. By letting them know you understand that they may be subject matter experts in a particular skillset, you are letting them know you would like to start a partnership with them where you can both help each other.

Building Relationships

After selling your mission, begin constructing relationships. When building relationships with these resources, strive to convince them that your intentions are to build a partnership that is mutually beneficial. Explain to them that by partnering up, you are both now able to offer mutual services to one another which will increase the versatility and skillsets of your organizations. The previous example includes the local real estate developers. Convincing them to let you check their house designs and structures makes them trust you, building that relationship with them.

Sharing Knowledge

Sharing what you know is the recipe to a continuous network flow. What information you and your team have should be communicated and passed on to the other agencies and people that you network with. What good is the knowledge or expertise you have on a subject if you are not willing to share it? The more you share information, the easier it becomes for you to keep building your network.

Remaining Open-Minded

The fire service is an ever-evolving business. This situation demands an open-minded person willing to incorporate these changes to remain relevant in the area. For example, suppose you, as the training officer knew of an old way of handling an emergency in the community. However, a new standard or tactic has been introduced. A good training officer should have an open mind to new approaches, tactics, and standards.

Following the Networking Process

Better Vision

The more you network, the easier it is for you to understand the fire department's vision. For example, your initial vision may be ensuring community safety. Despite its excellent vision, it fails to address the necessities, including how to achieve it and which personnel to incorporate it. Networking allows you to understand the changing environment and what it means to enable community safety. It lets you know which bodies to keep close to and what training to incorporate to make your firefighters more prepared to tackle emergencies. As a result, your vision becomes better training to ensure that each firefighter has the right skills and knowledge to be more responsive in emergencies to ensure community safety.

More Prepared

Networking allows the fire department to have measures to tackle different issues that may arise. For example, if you have a neighboring department who has the equipment and skillset to provide technical rescue services, it would be advantageous to reach out to them and train with them. By setting up training sessions with that department, your team can learn the basics of how to use their equipment properly. The truth is that if there is a call in your first due for a technical rescue, you will most likely be requesting that department on mutual aid. Being as your team has trained with them, you both are able to double the efforts to mitigating the scene better. This also increases the relationships, now that you have trained together, you now have established a rapport with them. That rapport helped exchange the expectations and strengthened the mutual trust between both departments.

Stay Current

Networking also ensures that training officers remain current with tactics and standards. Agencies like the NFPA are responsible for creating new standards that are often incorporated into curriculum, which a training officer should be aware of these updates and apply them as needed in your training program.

Challenges of Networking

Networking Stigma

Over the past few years, social media has created a negative perception amongst fire departments. Between the bullying sites and the clowns who take selfies with a member of the community's worst day ever in the background, social media has been abused and negatively impacted the importance of networking. However, the flipside is, if used properly and for good cause, social media can be a great tool for a training officer to use to strengthen their department. For example, social media allows interactions of people from different parts of the world, allowing them to exchange ideas and information. Platforms allowing this process include Facebook, Instagram, and LinkedIn. Furthermore, I live in Pennsylvania and have friends in different American states, including Oklahoma, New York, Tennessee, California, and many others. I also have friends in other countries like Japan and Italy. We cannot meet physically daily, but social media allows us to communicate and exchange ideas. This communication improves my ability to train firefighters because it introduces me to concepts I never knew.

Training officers with a negative perception of social media are unable to take advantage of the benefits associated with being able to connect and share information. Social media is free, but more training officers are reluctant to use it because they perceive these platforms as unfavorable. In some ways, they are right. Social media is sensitive. It only takes one person from a fire department to ruin its image.

For example, if a firefighter from a particular fire department makes a post on social media something that can be hateful or disrespectful in nature. There are times where members of the fire service will use social media as a method of "trolling" or bullying other first responders. If the posts are innocent in nature, there may be room for a lesson to be learned or even a laugh. However, this can also leak to the public, which will certainly paint a bad image of the fire department and its leadership amongst their stakeholders and customers. Such a situation makes social media sensitive, ensuring that people from that organization become cautious of what they post on these platforms.

Ego

As we've covered a couple of times in previous chapters, the phrase, "we have always done it that way" very much exists throughout the fire service. This annoying phrase is also used as an excuse when it comes to why training officers aren't networking. That attitude makes people complacent in their activities because they do not want to implement newer ideas. For example, if one suggests the fire department network with mutual aid partners, I assure you there will be people refusing that idea. Why? We have always done it that way. Similar to what we discussed in Chapter 4, Egoism ensures a close-minded approach because these types of training officers are reluctant to implement newer ideas because they prefer the older way of doing things.

How to Tackle These Challenges

Be More Open

An open mindset ensures that one does not understand egoism. The officer becomes interested in networking because they believe the process makes them see things differently. As a result, they can remain current, allowing them to comply with the different standards issued by agencies such as NFPA. An open-minded person will not use the phrase, "we have always done it that way" because it limits their ability to be more creative and apply measures that may be essential to their development.

Proper Leadership

A good leader influences others positively. A training officer is a leader. They should influence others positively and set the expectation that their firefighters value the importance of progressive training. Because they lead a group, they will have firefighters who follow their guidance, yet also have those that ignore them. As a result, they need to understand how to handle such issues.

There are four things that the leader can incorporate to ensure better leadership as a training officer. They include:

- Guidance
- Support
- Organization
- Direction

Guidance

Training officers should guide others because in truth there are many that consider them their role models. If you are the training officer and you practice good networking skills with outside agencies, your firefighters will emulate those same traits, allowing them to network with firefighters from other fire departments.

Support

Training officers should support networking. They should be the frontrunners of this activity because of the very nature of their position, which is to introduce versatility in the multiple disciplines needed for a strong training program. The more they network with other fire departments, the higher the likelihood of them engaging in training together. As a result, they execute tactics in the field better.

Organization

Organization involves forming ways to reach different people. For example, the training officer can construct local outreach programs to allow firefighters to communicate with various people from the community. It will be an excellent learning process because firefighters and the training officer will know which areas of the community may need more attention.

Direction

Direction is ensuring that everyone receives the correct instructions in activity execution. Training officers should instruct firefighters on what measures to incorporate to be more compliant with networking. They should address issues like egoism and stigmatization and how they may potentially impact their ability to network. Instructing them how to conduct themselves to make them less likely to fall victim to such issues is vital to their success.

Summary

Good leadership entails four critical processes: **guidance**, **support**, **organization**, and **direction**. These elements enable a training officer to issue better advice to firefighters regarding networking, allowing them to create better relations with mutual aid partners. As a result, the firefighters understand why networking is important to their training and the fire department. They also understand why egoism and networking stigma are barriers to networking and why they should avoid them. As the training officer, you should be vigilant in addressing this issue to ensure that firefighters represent the department's image correctly.

Training Budgets

Budget cuts are worse today because of the current economic state. The inflation rate is increasing, making it difficult to access services at the usual rate. For example, wood prices are growing massively, putting the fire department's activities at risk. Fire departments depend on wood to make certain props used for training. With the increasing budget cuts, it becomes difficult for them to match the rising wood prices. Moreover, they should add more responsibility to their firefighters' making the props.

I had to tackle such an issue as a training officer. There were budget cuts at the time, leaving the only viable solution as the firefighters helped build training props over the summer. It was a tough call for me because the firefighters were already feeling the pain from the budget cuts. I was empathetic to their situation and worked hand and hand with them to finish building the props. Luckily, they appreciated that and were willing to assist me.

This situation is not the same for all training officers. Training officers have firefighters with different personalities. If my problem were to play out in other fire departments, some firefighters may reject the proposal, putting training in a difficult spot. In other situations, the training officer could force the firefighters to do an action, something that would lead to a hostile environment. Regardless, the case indicates the impact of budget cuts on training and the fire department.

Networking offers a solution to budget cuts. For example, fire departments can combine their training to allow them to share their props. There may be situations where the local lumber yard or contractor who operates within your response area will donate lumber and other building materials. By reaching out to your neighboring areas, this can help secure the much-needed amenities to build training props for your organization. In those cases, you may use your firefighters to make props from that wood. That not only helps build better training resources, but also develops cohesion amongst the team from them taking ownership on a project like that by building it together. In the short term, the activity may ensure they cope with budget cuts, but it may positively impact training in the long term. Firefighters who train together, work together. Making them more efficient when responding to emergencies.

The 3 Pillars of Networking

Before learning about the networking pillars, the foundation is important. The foundation incorporates good cheerleading. Training officers should be the frontrunners of cheerleading networking as they create relations with others. If the training officer has an ego about networking, other firefighters may refuse to network because they assume the training officer is right. This situation makes it vital for the training officer to adopt the four key leadership elements: guidance, support, organization, and direction. Those steps will allow compliance from other members because they want to imitate their leaders.

 # Mentor Network

This network includes a trusted partner or advisor (preferably an unbiased third party). The individual should put the department's developmental needs as a priority. Sometimes, departments employ someone with a conflict of interest, making them put their needs ahead of the department. As a result, resource allocation becomes an issue, limiting the department's ability to enjoy networking benefits. Advisors with close relations to the department may be biased toward how they perform their activities. They may have a conflict of interest, making them ignore the bird's eye view. As a result, networking can become an issue because the department will not incorporate relations to assist them but those that satisfy the advisor's view. This situation makes it critical for fire departments to understand which type of advisors to employ and those who should stay away from their functional assessment.

Focus on the Bigger Picture

You want to recruit someone who is able to assess your program from all angles. Similar to how an incident commander will conduct a "360", the person who you invite to assess the functionality of your department should metaphorically do the same. By visualizing things using the bird's eye view approach, this unbiased person should be able to recognize any potential gaps, while also complimenting your strengths. This should only help you find ways to strengthen your department's training program.

Roles the Trusted Advisor Assumes

Awareness

The trusted advisor should understand the department's policies. Understanding these policies will enable them to review and spot any changes needed to ensure better performance. For example, the trusted advisor can notice a potential issue with how the engine company operations went. As the advisor, they can raise that issue with the training officer and suggest how they should perform better. This situation leads to developing an awareness for the training officer, allowing them to formulate ways in which they can address the issue.

Training Policies and Reports

The trusted advisor should look at training reports, including the number of injuries suffered during the training and the general training format. This situation allows them to decide how to better the condition and if immediate measures are necessary to remedy it. In some cases, the advisor may see it wise for the department to incorporate newer training equipment to help enhance the skills performed during training.

Incident Reports

The trusted advisor should look at incident reports to see the types of emergencies the department responds to. As a result, they may offer suggested techniques in how the department can prepare for those emergencies. For example, the incident report can indicate types of emergencies and the frequencies of those emergencies. Moreover, the incident reports can show a lack of proper documentation being noted in the reports. In such a situation, the advisor may recommend that the training officer introduce leadership training or proper report writing and data collection methods training. This situation helps for better performance both in training and during emergencies, as well as exposes the need for proper documentation for incident reporting.

Staffing

The trusted advisor should also look at staffing requirements. This situation includes understanding the worker output of the department. For example, the advisor can find out the number of firefighters usually sent by the department during an emergency. The advisor can then evaluate if this number is sufficient to handle emergencies by looking at the department's performance during an incident. If the performance is poor, they can recommend more staffing to assist in the efficiency of emergency mitigation as well as prevention of firefighter injuries that may be caused due to an inadequate number of firefighters responding to an emergency.

In other situations, the issue may be recruitment because of the budget cuts. These situations make it crucial for the trusted advisor to use their networking skills to help remedy the situation. This action can be through combining efforts from different fire departments or liaising with the appropriate bodies to see whether more funds can be available for recruitment.

Actions after Trusted Advisor performs their Duties

After Action Report

The department should create an after-action report to establish whether the organization is complying with the advice recommended by the trusted advisor. The information allows them to investigate whether the activities are going as planned or if there are more immediate changes needed to negate a potential issue. The training officer should write the report and provide general feedback regarding the change process.

LT Miller conducts an A.A.R. after a drill.

Setting up a Drill to Perform Actions

Training officers should oversee different drills to see whether firefighters are complying with the stipulations indicated by the trusted advisor. If there was an issue with the engine company operations, the training officer should ensure they issue better guidelines in that activity.

 # Resource Network

This network includes individuals from the government and the local community.

The resource network should have people from different public sectors. This situation ensures diversity because people will have different skillsets that will benefit from networking. For example, by networking with car dealerships who sell electric vehicles, the training officer can obtain relevant information from motor vehicle experts about the impact of electrified vehicle emergencies.

How to Reach the Community

Fire departments employ different ways of reaching people within society. These ways to connect may include public events such as an open house at the fire station, where local businesses such as real estate agencies, car dealerships, and many others may attend.

Open House at the Fire Department

Hosting an open house at your fire station can be a way to engage with your local community while marketing your mission. This serves as a networking platform, connecting with community members and their families who are not only stakeholders but also potential links to local businesses, politicians, and other influential opportunities. Positive experiences at the fire station can encourage these individuals to support your department, either through donations or resources that enhance your training programs. For instance, a visitor who owns a salvage yard could offer cars for vehicle extrication drills, providing practical training scenarios. Hosting an open house can an effective method to network with the community. By doing so, you create a pathway to improve your training program through community engagement and resourceful networking. This situation allows firefighters to interact with children and their parents. It involves a process that lets the department build relationships with the community.

FF Wortman, LT Rindt, FF Miller & FF Kvilesz do a great job of marketing the mission.

Local Real Estate Agencies

With the new methods of housing construction and materials used, training officers must network with real estate developers. They can create appointments with them before potential buyers come to see the house to allow them to study the housing structure. By doing this, firefighters can better prepare understand what to do if there are emergencies because they know what the house structure is.

Seeing this house before potential buyers buy is essential because the house becomes a private entity that a training officer may not have access to after purchase.

Local Dealerships

These car dealerships have sales people and maintenance personnel. The maintenance personnel know more about vehicles, making them the right people to teach firefighters about them. Because of the switch from gas vehicles to electric cars, there is a gap that leaves many firefighters poorly equipped to handle emergencies related to electric cars. They can learn more about these vehicles by consulting with the maintenance personnel.

Hotels

Pre-planning is a vital activity in hotels. I remember a time in 2005 when I was a firefighter in New Jersey we responded to a report of a fire in an eleven-story hotel, so by definition a high-rise. Over the five years that I was a member of the fire department; I never did a pre-plan on that building. When we arrived on scene, we did everything textbook (proper apparatus positioning, high-rise pack, tools, PPE, hooking up to the standpipe, securing a water supply, etc.). When we got to the fire room, we had to force the door and as soon as we did so the hallway was instantly charged with smoke.

As we advanced the line and attempted to knock down the fire, the water pressure became low, so I had to find out why that was the case. I rectified the situation and, on my way back, I heard a woman yell out "HELP, HELP!" I quickly adjusted gears and followed the yells from the woman so I could connect with her and get her out.

As I brought the woman to the stairwell and passed her off to another Firefighter, I was greeted with more people who were lost in the smoke-filled hallway yelling for help. After it was all said and done, we discovered that eleven people needed our help, something we did not know because we thought that everybody had already evacuated safely. I did not know that floors 7 through 11 dumped off into the 6th floor where occupants were to leave one stairwell and travel down the hallway on the 6th floor to another stairwell which would then bring them to the lobby. Had I have been through that building before, or my team had done better preplanning, we might have known the layout of that building and ensured that the building was properly evacuated prior to forcing the door to the fire room and filling the hallway with smoke. Luckily, we managed to get everyone out.

It was an experience that taught me the benefits of pre-planning. As training officers, we should pre-plan any building to familiarize ourselves with its environment. It may seem like a tedious process at first, but it is crucial during emergencies.

 **Training Network**

This network includes the following individuals:

Mutual Aid Partners

They include:

- Police departments
- Fire departments
- First aid squads (EMS)
- HazMat response teams

Invite Others to Play in Your Sandbox

The fire department should invite other fire departments within the region to training. This will be vital to build relationships and understand each other's skillsets. The more they train together, the easier it will be to ensure better performance in the field. Far too many times are we afraid to invite others to join us in training, whether it is a fear of exposing inadequate performance or just pure ego. There is no excuse why you shouldn't be training with the same people who you will be operating with during an emergency.

Dodgeball Team

As you develop your network you are essentially picking your dodgeball team. Your dodgeball team should consist of the groups and people mentioned throughout this chapter. Ensuring that your dodgeball team has the right players is of the highest importance.

Your dodgeball team should comprise of the following qualities.

- Passionate individuals
- Motivators
- People brought in to improve culture
- People with a specialized skillset

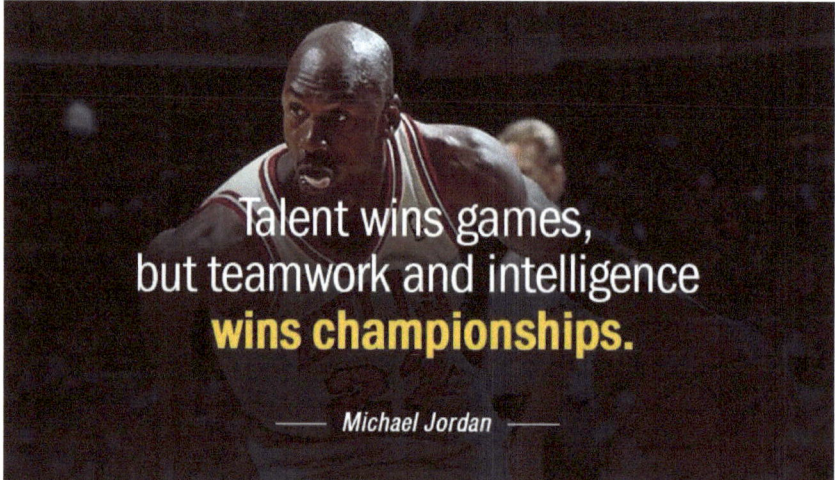

Passionate people are important because you want to make sure that the people on your team love training and developing their organization as much if not more than you do. Motivators are important because they have an ability to motivate the other members of the network to be more involved and bought into building the network. Bringing outsiders in will help improve the culture. Giving the outside perspective of what can be improved will help others see things they have missed over the years. Lastly, ensuring people have a specialized skillset helps your team be more diverse and assists in the growth of proficiency in the services your team provides.

The key takeaway here is to start communicating with your people and your stakeholders. Build a network with those people so you can create a good training program that delivers high quality services to the public. Remember, it's easy, it all starts with a handshake and a smile.

A VIEW FROM EXPERIENCE

By: Steve Hamilton
Assistant Chief, Fort Jackson (SC) Fire Department

Steven C. Hamilton has been a member of the fire service since 1996 and a law enforcement officer since 2010. He is an Air Force veteran, national speaker, published author, and respected instructor. Chief Hamilton has also served as a subject matter expert for the NFPA 3000 Active Shooter/Hostile Emergency Response (ASHER) standard. He is currently assigned to the training division for the Fort Jackson Fire Dept.

"The process of building relationships to provide or obtain resources, information, or technical expertise that is cyclical in nature and mutually beneficial in achieving goals and objectives."

A guiding concept to the handshake and a smile concept is to be open and available to *EVERYONE*. You should be willing to go the extra mile in your service delivery while engaging with your customer base. Calls for service are where we typically shine to our public. Their worse day is happening at lightning speed and your kindness, compassion, and empathy goes a long way in helping them cope with that experience. Have you ever had someone retell an unfortunate circumstance in which they had to call the fire department; a loved one passing, a fire, or a significant car wreck? In that, you may remember a particular recounting in which the actions of the responders resonate as much if not more than the incident itself. That's the impact personnel have on a daily basis. The incident becomes an opportunity to leave a significant impact and one that compliments you and your agency.

Creating a positive service delivery reputation compels others to want to help you and your agency in the unique ways they can. This can be the small business owner who lets you use their building during closed hours for training. It can also be the auto salvage yard owner who opens their doors on the weekends for you to conduct extrication training. Every interaction when you respond to a call is an opportunity to make a connection.

Calls for service are not our only interaction with the public where opportunities present themselves. In extending that handshake and a smile be sure to palm a business card along with it. It should become part of your normal introduction process. Handing over a card and saying, "Feel free to contact me anytime if there is ever anything I can do for you" is paramount to building a network. Be true in that statement. If and when that call comes, move mountains to help them in the ways in which you can. Coined, servant sacrifice, it's merely a willingness to sacrifice your time and energy to aid another. Doing so builds your reputation as someone who is going to go the extra mile to help another. Once built, the receivers will likely do the same for you when you call them for a favor.

The same rings true when meeting with fellow responders from other agencies. They may be next door in the adjoining jurisdiction, or they may be on the other side of the country. They may have knowledge or insight into struggles you have in your programs and processes. Struggles they have conquered and can aid you in overcoming yours. Proximity is of little consequence when trying to build your rolodex with contacts.

A handshake and a smile are all it takes to begin building relationships that become your network. Executing that concept should come from a place of subservience and be true in intention. Be willing to go the extra mile for Mrs. Smith with the same energy and vigor that you would for your idol or a fire service legend. Who they are should have little to do with how much time and effort you spend on being the answer. This is how you ring true to people and gain the reputation necessary to build a lasting and sustainable network.

Chapter 8
Training Program Development

This chapter will discuss how to develop an effective training program. This activity is essential to any fire department because of three key reasons:

- Detailing the Training

A firefighter's training should not be the same as that of a chief officer or a fire inspector. Each position should have its own unique training. For example, a firefighter's training will take longer than a chiefs because of the difference in experience and responsibilities. Whereas a chief should or would have disciplines that focused on budget training, incident command, leadership, administration, and policies and procedures training, while the firefighter would be more task driven with basic level operational skills coupled with technical skills that are duties commonly performed by the firefighter. This situation makes it ideal to have a proper training program that details each individual's training type.

- Documenting OTJ Injuries during Training: aka *CYA*

We live in a society where accidents happen to everyone. When an injury occurs to a firefighter during training, there will be measures implemented by the plan to ensure that there is compensation. This communication channel is important for the department because it communicates how it handles injuries sustained during training. The training officer should understand the importance of proper documentation, especially when it comes to on-the-job (OTJ) injuries sustained during training. This not only ensures the training officer covers their ass, but also allows the opportunity for introducing corrective measures and better safety practices to be implemented into training.

- Futuristic Plan

A training program should offer a futuristic advantage to the fire department because it lays down its mission and vision. As a result, the department sticks to working to ensure it achieves this vision and mission, a situation that allows them to be more progressive and proficient. Furthermore, the department can evaluate different measures in its training plan, including its needs assessment and SWOT, allowing it to comply with various regulations and standards, including agencies such as OSHA and state laws.

Training Program Development Process

When developing a training program, you should complete a series of steps to capture every piece of information. A training program is a detailed analysis of all training measures and laws demanded by different organizational bodies. As a training officer, you should refuse to ignore any step because of the above advantages.

These steps include:

- Needs Assessment
- Service delivery capabilities
- METLs (pronounced metals)
- Operational Requirements
- Crawl, walk, and run methodology
- SWOT Analysis
- Community Risk Assessment-Standard of Cover (CRA/SOC)

Beginning Part of The Training Program

Needs Assessment

Each fire department should conduct a needs assessment and the data collected from that needs assessment should be reflected in your training program. A good option for the framework of what a needs assessment should look like or how to conduct one could be referencing and familiarizing with the Center for Public Safety Excellence (CPSE) Fire and Emergency Services Self-Assessment Manual (FESSAM). In the FESSAM there are many relevant recommendations that each fire department could benefit from on how to properly navigate conducting a needs assessment.

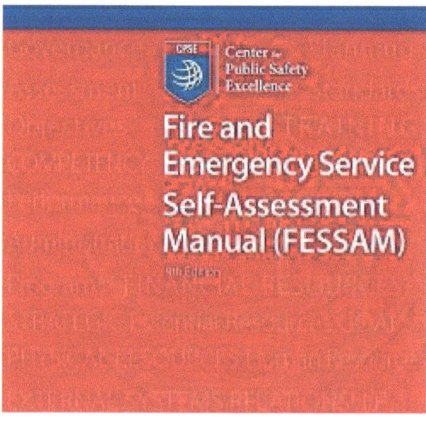

Functions of the FESSAM and Needs Assessment

How to Break Down Training

Training needs a specified flow to ensure firefighters understand what they are doing. The crawl, walk, and run methodology is standard in breaking down training. This model starts with a theoretical understanding of what the training involves and later continues to do the action practically. A more detailed explanation of the approach is available later in the chapter.

Performance Indicators

The Needs Assessment lays down the key performance indicators in fire department training. Moreover, these indicators include average completion time, class attendance rate, and the activity's pass or fail rate. Each indicator establishes a specific phenomenon for the training officer. For example, if the activity fail rate is very high, it may be a sign that the officer needs to change the training approach to incorporate more success. The training officer should be flexible in changing the training program to ensure positive performance indicators.

Standards & Regulations

The training program should comply with the standards and recommendations by OSHA, state laws, NFPA, and the community. The more it complies with such measures, the more it has validity and offers a sense of assurance to the community. Furthermore, such standards ensure that the fire department does not face unnecessary lawsuits.

Training Materials

The Needs Assessment indicates the significance of a training program having the materials required for each training. For example, if the training is focused on a structure fire, the training materials may include a building/facility that allows for firefighters to perform a structural drill in, smoke or fog machine, manikins, hoses, ladders, and much more. As a result, the training program should indicate these materials to allow firefighters to know the tools they are dealing with during drills.

Mission Statement

In order to truly capture what the program is about your training program should have a mission statement. The mission statement indicates what the department does, why it exists, the type of services offered, and its core values.

This first step includes formulating the mission and vision of the training program. Each component has its reasons, as explained below.

The mission is vital because:

- It explains why you exist
- It explains what you do
- The type of services you offer
- The fire department's core values

When formulating a mission statement, it is essential to include all these four components to ensure whoever reads it understands the mission.

Example of A Mission Statement

Our mission is to provide the best format that offers the technical knowledge needed for preparedness to [*your name*] fire department members through our core values: education, readiness, passion, and pride in training.

Vision

The vision is crucial because it enables the fire department to look to the future. As the department looks to the future, it becomes more proficient and progressive in performing its duties. The more progressive and proficient it is, the higher the chances of issuing better training to its firefighters.

Example of a Vision Statement

Our vision is to establish a seamless plan that offers the tools necessary to develop the future of [*your name*] fire department.

Summary of What You Do

The mission and vision statements are crucial to addressing the stakeholders and community. They understand the fire department's training, allowing them to be more confident during emergencies because they know firefighters will effectively perform their duties.

Example of Such a Summary

As a team of highly trained and dedicated professionals, our mission is to provide the highest standard of service to all who may seek our help. We are a service provider and stand ready to provide fire suppression, fire prevention, education, rescue services, and emergency medical services. We will faithfully provide these vital services promptly and safely to any person who resides in, works in, or visits [*community name*] and its surroundings.

Service Delivery Capabilities

When formulating these capabilities, it is vital to establish core subjects. After that, you can divide those cores into other disciplines, which the firefighters can train by different frequencies. In my fire department, we have what I call "the core four" they are as follows:

- Structural firefighting
- Hazardous materials
- Emergency medical services
- Technical rescue

Each core has its divisions in which it stipulates different training requirements. For example, the disciplines in structural firefighting can include drivers training, hose evolutions, search and rescue, as well as pre-incident planning. For each discipline, the training officer should indicate the operational requirements, frequency, and METLs.

Mission, Essential, Task, and Listings

Mission, Essential, Task, and Listings is abbreviated as METL's. When handling METLs, the training officer should formulate the frequency, which can be annually, semi-annually, quarterly, or monthly.

Each training should have a METL outlining the training mission, essentials, tasks, and listings. For example, in driver's training, the mission can be to ensure that firefighters understand how to handle vehicles during emergencies. The essentials can be the apparatus, the equipment on it, and fuel. Furthermore, the training officer should list these requirements in the training program. Each core should have its disciplines and METLs. The frequency is another aspect the training officer should list in the program, and this component is available in the next section, needs assessment.

Operational Requirements

Each discipline requires its operational requirements. For example, hazardous materials can have various disciplines like chemical exposure training, level suits training, reference materials, and meters training. These disciplines have various operational requirements, including having the correct gear and learning to safely mitigate the hazard. The equipment a firefighter may require in driver training can be completely different from hazardous materials. As a result, understanding these operational requirements becomes essential.

Crawl, Walk, and Run Methodology

After establishing the needs assessment, the training officer should specify the methodology they will use in their training. This methodology should be present in the training plan.

The Crawl Phase

This phase is where the classroom introduction happens. The training officer discusses the training with the firefighters and allows various conversations to happen. For example, if the training is on saws, the training officer explains how they use saws to cut open roofs for ventilation and how they can also use them to cut metal bar windows. The class should meet all requirements and curriculum standards as well as gain familiarization with the manufacturer's recommendations for use. For example, if the class is on saws, there are specific types of fuel and fuel mixes that some saws need to be operated properly. Items such as the fuel types are important to be part of the learning objectives during the crawl phase.

The Walk Phase

This phase involves the firefighters putting their hands on the materials. Because it is a saws class, the firefighters learn to change the blade, change the chain on the saw, and put bar oil if needed etc. The walk phase allows more interactive sessions with the materials to prepare the firefighters for the actual practice.

The Run Phase

This phase is where the firefighters practice using the equipment. In this instance, the firefighters participate in drills to use the saws. They can use them to cut metal bar windows or open roofs for ventilation. Practice prepares them for what skills they may need to perform during emergencies.

Suggestions for Distinctive Disciplines

Seasonal Training

In many parts of the country there are four distinct seasons, and with each comes different weather and temperature differences. Because of the season effects difference,

Training Program Development

the training officer should establish how to train the firefighters in preparation for the upcoming season. This training involves performing training following the seasons.

In my department when the winter is approaching, I will set specific topics such as carbon monoxide emergencies in September. This training prepares department members who have higher chances of responding to carbon monoxide poisoning during the winters because of the closed windows and the lighting of furnaces.

In other areas of the country there are fire departments who may face extreme winter seasons that include a mission to perform rescues in the snow. Training on victim removal in rural areas is important, but if the training only occurs during seasons when it is typically warm may result in one level of preparedness.

If your fire department has a mission where your firefighters may have to perform a rescue in the snow, then there should be training set specifically for that season. This helps the firefighters stay proficient in those skills while planning ahead on how to perform rescue scenarios in snow or ice.

Another example of something we do at my department during the winter months is set aside time for firefighters to train on apparatus driver/operator while using snow chains to see their performance on snowy or slippery road conditions. Driver/operator training is great throughout the year, but if you are also not training on driving for the change in the road conditions, you could potentially set yourself up for failure or worse injury. Due to the fact that fires don't take the winter off, we still respond to fires and other emergencies during the winter. Therefore, this example is important to those who have response areas with those conditions to ensure their people are being trained in that skillset as well, being that it is a completely different method of driving.

Seasonal training ensures that firefighters revisit their basic skillset every three months, which is usually the duration of each season. By incorporating this training regime, training officers can ensure that the firefighters develop proficiency in specific skills every three months allowing for efficiency in work performance while building preparedness for the potential emergencies they will respond to during those seasons.

Stigmatic Training

This training is typically but not limited to subjects such as mental health and suicide awareness. These types of training topics are rarely in conversations among people because of their delicate nature. It is high time that people recognize the need for such programs, especially with the increasing number of suicides within the fire department. Firefighting is a difficult job, and without the correct mindset, it is easy to fall victim to suicide. It, therefore, lies with the training officer to incorporate such training to ensure that firefighters understand how difficult their job can be on various occasions.

The delivery of this type of training can be difficult. Some are either uncomfortable, while others may not take it seriously because they lack both sympathy and empathy. Regardless of the case, the training officer needs to set an environment where that topic is discussed. A good and healthy lecture with the firefighters will help them understand how to help prevent this reality, or even potentially save one of your own's life. This training may come at a time when someone within your own department might be dealing with some stuff. The comfort and fact that you showcase that you value this topic may encourage those people to open up and ask for help. I worked in two departments now where we discussed this very topic and two different occasions, we had people come up to us afterwards and admit they were ready to "check out." You see, this topic is serious, and its importance cannot be dismissed. We literally saved someone's life twice just by talking about this topic.

The truth is, no one understands us better than us. By taking it seriously and sharing our own stories will help others feel comfortable to share theirs and in essence "purge." Firefighters love to tell stories about calls they were on; we just never normalize getting the bad stuff off our chest too. The training officer needs to recognize this and establish an environment where the entire team feels comfortable and takes this topic serious.

The frequency of this training depends on the training officer. They should ensure that their training remedies the increasing number of suicides among firefighters. Furthermore, the training should include various guiding and counseling sessions that allow firefighters to express their concerns. It is the training officer's responsibility to not only champion this topic but to cheerlead it in a way that the firefighters are receptive to it and embrace it willingly. This is done through proper research coupled with the earlier mentioned attributes of sympathy and empathy.

SWOT Analysis

SWOT stands for **Strengths, Weaknesses, Opportunities**, and **Threats**. The training officer should establish each component and how to handle them to be more advantageous to the department.

> **Test Your Understanding**

A training officer does a SWOT analysis and establishes various weaknesses and threats to the fire department's training. The officer decides to turn all weaknesses and threats into strengths.

Is this a viable approach by the training officer?

- Yes
- No

The answer is no. As a training officer, you should understand that turning all weaknesses and threats into strengths is challenging. The environment is constantly changing, which may turn the department's strengths into weaknesses and vice versa. If your goal is to change all threats or weaknesses into strengths, it may present a situation where that is all you are doing, limiting the positive impact you could have on training.

A training officer should know that time and resources are factors that many fire departments lack. As a result, instead of changing all threats to strengths, the training officer should work on ensuring these threats remain dormant. Conducting the SWOT helps expose what the gaps are and what types of challenges can pose a threat to the success of the training program. Ensuring awareness of those is the most important factor, turning them into strengths is secondary. Where the officer can change them to strengths, they can do so. The officer should also understand the value of having a training committee who will be tasked with the purpose of conducting the SWOT analysis. As a result, decision-making on such essential issues will not be a one-person burden but a collective initiative.

What A SWOT Analysis Entails

A SWOT analysis involves all the department's Strengths, Weaknesses, Opportunities, and Threats. The training committee should list all these elements before conducting a complete analysis of how they will manage them. Furthermore, the SWOT analysis should take a three-way methodology: short, mid, and long-term. The short-term approach is annual, the mid-term is after three years, and the long-term plan is after every five years. When evaluating the SWOT analysis in the long term, the analysis may be different because some strengths may be weaknesses and vice versa. If the SWOT analysis is the same after five years, there is a high likelihood that the training committee will not do an excellent job in the analysis.

It is worth noting that the change expected should not be a complete turnover. The SWOT analysis does not need to be completely different. The process may create many unanswered questions if it is entirely different. The training committee should see to it that there are some changes to the analysis because of the ever-changing environment.

The training committee should list how it intends to ensure proficiency and progress in the long term. If the SWOT analysis indicates more weaknesses and threats than strengths and opportunities, the committee should explain how they will handle this situation. For example, the committee can say it will work on their opportunities and turn them into strengths. If there is an opportunity to lower costs by making props themselves, it can implement that as a requirement. As a result, the opportunity becomes a strength allowing it to have a bigger budget.

On the other hand, if the weakness is inadequacy in training materials, the department can improve its networking with other fire departments. As a result, they can indulge in the same training, allowing them to use the equipment of other fire departments. This situation turns their weakness of deficiency in training materials into a strength. These steps of how the committee intends to work on their strengths, weaknesses, opportunities, and threats should be available in the training program.

Qualities a T.O. Needs to Form a Training Program

Understand SWOT

The previous section indicates the value of knowing SWOT and how to use it. The training officer should know this function to allow them to make better decisions regarding training. For example, instead of wanting to turn all the department's weaknesses into strengths, the officer can decide to make these weaknesses dormant. The officer should only work on turning weaknesses into strengths if the time and resources allow. If they do not, the officer should stick to ensuring that the weaknesses remain dormant.

Understand Service Delivery Capabilities

As a training officer, you should know why these capabilities are essential to a training program. For example, each capability should have various disciplines in which the training officer establishes a frequency in which firefighters train. For instance, there should be multiple disciplines like driver training and pre-incident planning if it is a structural firefighting capability. After identifying these disciplines, the training officer should indicate the frequency in which they intend to practice the driver's training and pre-incident planning. A knowledgeable training officer should know these processes and insist firefighters adhere to them.

Understand the Need to Breakdown Training

The training officer should know the importance of breaking down training and how to do it. This chapter is instrumental if you are a training officer and do not know how to break down training. By following the suggested steps can help you develop a successful training program. As a training officer, you should understand what all these steps entail and why it is essential to include them in the training program.

Regular Updates

A training officer should continuously evaluate the training program. After forming it, you should not ignore it because policies and standards are constantly updating. As a result, you should incorporate these changes into the training program to comply with these standards. Furthermore, it ensures the training program is up-to-date with the latest training procedures. For example, with the increasing technology, house designs are changing, making it crucial for firefighters to know them. A good way of achieving this outcome is by complying with the standards issued by state laws and other relevant organizations.

The issue with the house designs leads us to community risk assessment. Why is this assessment vital, and what does it entail? These are some of the questions the next section will address.

Community Risk Assessment/Standard of Cover (CRA/SOC)

The training committee should understand its community before building its training program. The significance of the fire department is to offer safety to its community and surroundings. As a result, they should know the community structure and the type of buildings present to know the risk.

Some of examples of things the department should know include:

- If there are chemical plants in the area
- If there are hospitals in the area
- The type of buildings in the area
- If there are daycare centers or schools in the area
- The area's history regarding active shooter

Understanding these elements allows the training officers to know what training to target most and how they prepare for emergencies. For example, if the area has many active shooter cases, the training officer should train firefighters on handling such an issue. The issue of researching active shooter cases is a sensitive one but one that the fire department should recognize. We live in a society where these incidents are rampant, making it ideal for firefighters to know how to deal with the situation.

Population Changes During Certain Times

Some regions are tourist attractions, meaning that during specified times of the year, there will be a high number of people in that area, a situation that may lead to emergencies. Other regions may host global sporting events during a given time, making it ideal for the fire department to have extreme preparedness.

The Evacuation Procedures

Once the fire department understands the population's demands, it should establish what evacuation procedures to follow to ensure community safety. For example, if the population is extremely high, then the situation means there will be an increased need for training to focus on evacuation demands. Due to the increased number of residents needing to be evacuated, this can become overwhelming if not practiced in advance. From those training sessions, the training officer and leadership should develop an action plan to handle such an emergency.

Importance of Conducting Community Research

Better Preparedness

The training officer can incorporate specified training for the firefighters. For example, if community research identifies that the area has many chemical plants, it is likely to be more prone to a hazardous materials emergency. As a result, training officers should train firefighters on handling such incidents. The training plan, therefore, should incorporate training on hazardous materials mitigation to promote community safety.

Networking

Community research allows the fire department to identify other fire departments. As a result, they can work together in training, allowing them to be more effective in their duties. In the long run, networking can also help them save on costs and focus on issuing better training. The training officer should incorporate these elements in the training plan to make stakeholders aware of how the training works. Also, it lets firefighters know that their training happens with other fire departments, allowing them to build on their team spirit.

Networking also happens between fire departments and other businesses, including real estate agencies. For example, if the training officer wants the schematics of a given house, they can liaise with the real estate developer to have the designs and/or floor plans. As a result, they build on that relationship allowing them to receive updates in modern housing. These changes allow them to have better training programs because they will incorporate training on handling such houses during emergencies.

Building the Training Program

When building this program, the training officer should understand what elements to incorporate. There are numerous elements the officer should include:

List of Instructors

The training program should have the names of all the instructors overseeing the training. The list is vital because it captures who the SMEs (subject matters experts) are and what services they bring to the table that help strengthen your training program.

Mission and Vision Statements

A training program should have these statements. Each statement should have all the information that pertains to it, as discussed in the first section of this chapter. The training should adhere to these statements, and the training officer will be responsible for demanding that all firefighters stick to achieving the fire department's mission and vision.

How to Attend Training

The training program should indicate the materials needed for the training and the standards the firefighters should follow before attending. Furthermore, the firefighters should know which type of training they will be doing and how they can request it. All these stipulations should be available within the training program to ensure that each firefighter knows what drill they will be doing and for what duration.

Person Overseeing the Training

Because of the different instructors involved, the training program should indicate the instructor during each training session. The situation allows the firefighters to communicate with the person responsible for that specific training.

List of Hours during Training

Each training should have a stipulated period attached to it. For example, if firefighters need various training to complete their standards, they should have a specified period. The training officer should know that each training is different, and as a result, they should be aware that some training activities may take longer than others. Therefore, they should indicate the time allocated to each training course.

Number of People in the Training Committee

The training committee is responsible for overseeing the formulation of the entire training program. As a result, the program should indicate the number of people in the committee as it allows any pressing issue to go to them. Also, the training committee oversees the training, making it essential to have the list of names of those on the committee.

How CRA/SOC, Needs Assessment, and SWOT Works

After undertaking the phases in developing the training program, the training committee should include all the stages. For example, the CRA/SOC should identify what risks are present in the community and the training allocated to negate these risks. Also, the SWOT analysis should indicate the department's strengths, weaknesses, opportunities, and threats and how it intends to maintain proficiency and progressiveness.

Level of Training

The training program should indicate which training is available for various people, including firefighters, fire inspectors, company officers, and chief officers. The training program should have these tiers to ensure that each person is working towards the training need for their position.

Training Objectives

The training program should list the target for each training. For example, if the training is on saws, the target can ensure that firefighters know how to use the saws to cut open roofs for ventilation and metal bar windows. If such objectives are present for each training, it makes it easier for firefighters to understand why they are doing a given training.

Training METLs

The training program should include each training METL and the annual requirements for each training. For example, if the training is about driver training, there should be a comprehensive list of driver/operator responsibilities such as but not limited to, driving, pumping, apparatus positioning, emergency vehicle operator's course (EVOC), etc. This will ensure that each firefighter has benchmarks that they know they need to train on.

SMART Objectives

SMART relates to **specific, measurable, achievable, relevant,** and **time-bound** objectives. The objectives indicated by the training program should have these five characteristics to allow the firefighters to know they are realistic targets. It also shows that the training program complies with the mission and vision statements.

- **S**pecific: The topic of training is specific to the mission needs or to the goals of the fire department.
- **M**easurable: The training can be measured through the length of content, or the level of steps and goals needed to ensure quality delivery and successful outcome of the topic is achieved.
- **A**chievable: Training is something that is not set up for failure but set up for success.
- **R**elevant: There is a specific and justified purpose for the training.
- **T**ime-bound: The training evolution does not go over the learning and attention time. Firefighters can focus and retain the information offered.

Reporting Injuries During Training

The training program should indicate the steps that any person injured during training should follow. This procedure allows the fire department to develop corrective actions to prevent future incidents from occurring.

Career Department

If your organization is a career department, the training program should indicate its expenses. These expenses include items such as but not limited to:

- Materials
- Tuition
- Staffing

Collaborative Training

The training program should indicate whether some training will happen with other fire departments. Collaborative training should occur if the fire departments are within the same region to allow firefighters to handle emergencies correctly. Such outcomes should be present in the training program.

Other things the training program can include are:

- Career advancement schools
- Expenses incurred
- Importance of After-Action Report

Repetition Training

Once you've developed your training program that meets your organization's mission needs. You need to layout the frequencies of training events. Due to the mission need coupled with the after-action information gathered from past training events, the training officer should incorporate repetition training of those topics and events.

Repetition training is important because it helps build off of the gaps exposed during previous training events. It is also important because the brain is a file cabinet, so therefore over time there is only a certain amount of up-to-date knowledge that will be retained in the brain. A reasonable example of this is technical rescue. Technical rescue efforts can be a perishable skill; therefore, it is important to have repetition of specific topics built into the frequencies of your training program.

If the need for your firefighters to retain the knowledge, skills, and abilities is every 6 months so they maintain proficiency in those topics, then the training officer should ensure their training program meets that need. If the training officer fails to have a level of repeated topics the firefighters may forget the specific skills and operations needed to be executed during a technical rescue emergency and therefore may be subject to failure in performing the needed tasks to mitigate that emergency.

As time goes on our brains will essentially push the older information in the back of the file cabinet and have the latest information at the very front. Because of this notion, repetition training should be a part of your training program, this ensures that information is always fresh and at the front of the firefighter's file cabinet (their brain) and therefore, ready to be accessed at any given emergency.

The takeaway here is that if you are a training officer you should ensure that there is room throughout your training program for repetition training. The safety and proficiency in the skills performed during emergencies is the main objective and justification of why routine, repetition, and meaningful frequency training is important. After all, we train everyday so we can perform like championship-style firefighters during emergencies.

A VIEW FROM EXPERIENCE

By: Scott Little
Fire Chief, Manheim Township (PA) Fire Rescue

Scott Little has 22 years of experience spans across federal, state, and local agencies which includes roles as chief fire officer, incident commander, company officer, fire and emergency services instructor, hazardous materials team leader, technical rescuer, and structural/airport firefighter. He has served in a variety of fire and emergency services positions including operations, training, and administrative management. He was recently the Fire Chief for the Lancaster City (PA) Bureau of Fire from May 2018 until his appointment to Fire Chief with Manheim Township. He also serves as a First Sergeant in the Pennsylvania Air National Guard, 193d Special Operations Medical Group, 193d Special Operations Wing, Harrisburg International Airport, Middletown, PA.

Be detailed. Be intentional. Be focused.

Be Detailed: Develop a Playbook

As the Training Officer you will be tasked with leading the most important aspect of every fire department. It's up to you to limit the noise and be self-disciplined to be focused on continuous improvement and development of your team. Remember the why behind your personal goals and reasons to be a Training Officer, block out the noise from the cheap seats, and stay focused on building the best team you can.

Being resilient is critical for anyone in a Training Officer position because you will find yourself at times doubting the playbook based on those that don't have the same level of passion or commitment to improving the department and themselves for one reason or another. Many times, this will be because they have grown into a space of comfort and now don't want to change, or have you found out what little knowledge or experience they truly have.

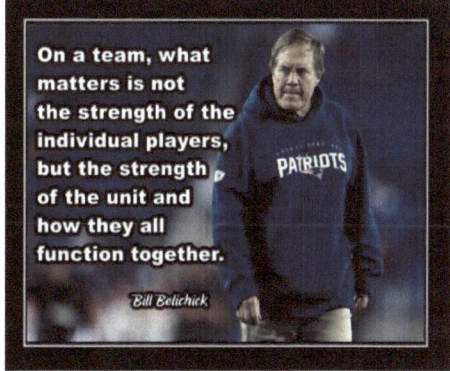

It's up to you to motivate them, push them, and lead them through this mindset change. You will set the standard for them to be successful, and ultimately reignite their love for the profession. It's tough work but must be done. You have been put in this position because someone else sees something in your ability to make change or improve the organization.

Think of your position as a sports team coach; what is it you want out of the team?

- Wins
- Meeting the Goals Set Personally and as a Team
- Recognize Personal Achievements
- Total Team Concept and Effort
- High Performance out of everyone

As the coach, you need to develop and implement the playbook. Make sure everyone on the team understands these simple yet important parts of the playbook.

- The why behind the playbook
- What is expected of each team member and how they are vital to the success of the playbook
- How the playbook will make the total team successful
- Reinforce everyone has a piece of this playbook
- It's not just the Chief's book

Don't do it alone, appoint an assistant coach or committee to help drive conversation, be open, be honest, and be inclusive.

What is it you want to do? What services do you provide? What level of training do you want for the team? What is the timeline to achieve success? What are the overall goals?

Set goals that are realistic for each member

- Meet with each member – find out what they want to achieve
- Use a timeline that lays out the training for each member
- Reward and recognition when they achieve these goals

Set goals that are realistic for the total team

- Team members goals
- Training Hours based on individual goals and as a team
- Reward and recognition when goals are achieved

Be Intentional: Know the Playbook

As a Training Officer you will be tasked to lead the most important aspect of every fire department.

We all know it should be at the forefront of fire department priorities, but not everyone wants to make the intentional commitment to training and continuous improvement. Some of the infamous quotes:

- Why do I have to do that again, I already did it once
- I don't want to
- It's too hot out
- It's too cold out
- Why do I need to know that? we will never use that

Training is the keystone that makes or breaks every fire department. Think of it as a sports team; manage and demand intentional action every day by members of your team. You are the manager and it's your responsibility to ensure everyone knows the playbook.

Make training a part of everyday activity. It doesn't have to be a long, drawn-out process but make it intentional and impactful to your crew.

Like a sports team, make sure you are practicing the plays and reviewing the playbook. Everyone needs to know their part and play calls. The last thing you should want is your crew learning the play (technique) once they arrive at the emergency incident. They need to be ready and come off the fire truck ready to execute the play and be successful.

Design your training plan in a way that breaks down the required skills on a monthly, quarterly, semi-annually, or annual basis.

Sample:

Subject	Frequency	Skill Level
SCBA Confidence Course	Semi-Annual	Active Interior Firefighters
Mayday Procedures	Quarterly	All Active Firefighters
Hazardous Materials Refresher	Annual	All Active Firefighters
Facility Walkthrough	Monthly	All Active Firefighters

Be Focused: Know Your Team on Any Given Sunday

Keep the playbook off the shelf. Keep it fresh and continue to always look for new ideas. Practice, Practice, Practice.

It takes a village to achieve positive results. The fire service is no different. To see these results, you will need to at times let it go, yes, I said it, LET IT GO! This will be tough and challenging because you will want to react but blocking out the noise from the cheap seats by surrounding yourself with like-minded professionals will keep you mentally, physically, and spiritually focused. Remember this is about them…the public in which we all pledged to protect and serve.

We cannot lose sight of the real reason we entered this profession. Helping others and making a positive impact in our local communities.

Stay focused on the total team, be inclusive, ask for feedback, and be honest about the work you and the committee are doing.

You have an entire network of like-minded fire service instructors willing to assist you and provide guidance – don't think you need to do this work alone. Reach out, ask questions, and remain positive – they (the community) are counting on you.

Chapter 9

Quality vs. Quantity

There is a common misconception when it comes to firefighter training regarding training hours. Many training officers get stuck with that "deer-in-the-headlights" look when you suggest that their programs should be more about the quality of the training being delivered and less on the quantity of hours per each training session. Over the years my experience as a training officer I have learned this important detail when it comes to firefighter training, and that has the value of having a training program that meets quality expectations. It does not have to incorporate many hours for it to be effective. In many instances, training should not take long hours because it will end up being ineffective. For example, if the training today is about saws, let the training meet the quality expectations. First, the training officer should incorporate the crawl-walk-run methodology, allowing firefighters to learn a new activity for each step. The crawl phase can entail the firefighters learning about the theoretical aspects of saws in class. Next, they put their hands on the saws, allowing them to learn how to change the blade and exchange the oil. Lastly, they incorporate drills to know how to use the saws to cut open roofs for ventilation.

These steps match the quality expectations needed for training. Unfortunately, many fire departments I have worked for incorporate quantity instead of quality training. They may focus too much on the theoretical aspects of saw training, making firefighters inefficient in handling emergencies related to saw training. Yes, the outcome may be that a firefighter has many training hours on their certification, but it means nothing if they cannot practically implement it into their jobs.

This situation brings the question of whose role it is to ensure that training programs are not quantity driven. It is the role of everyone in the fire department. The fire chiefs should set the organization's tone and demand that training meet quality expectations. Quality training demands that programs teach the required knowledge at the most appropriate time. This time should not be too long because most hours will be ineffective.

Test Your Understanding

A training officer is supposed to train their firefighters on structural firefighting. They understand that this training is essential for every firefighter and decide the best approach is to incorporate more training hours. Furthermore, some agencies require a minimum number of hours of training to be completed annually.

For example, an agency sets the requirements for each firefighter to meet a minimum of 120 training hours annually. The training officer decides to incorporate more theoretical classes to meet the expectations of the minimum standards.

Do quality standards drive this training?

- Yes
- No

The answer is No. The minimum standards indicate that training hours should be 120 annually, but it does not specify which training. As a training officer, you are a leader, and you should realize that as a leader, everybody expects you to make the right call. I am not saying that you are to ignore all the minimum requirements because there are some which can be meaningful and relevant to the mission. In this case, making firefighters sit for exceeded hours just because you want to comply with minimum standards will make you a bad training officer.

This situation requires experience. Yes, I said experience. We learned this concept in the first topic, and I described why experience is crucial for every training officer. The experience will allow the officer to make the right call and demand that training hours be shortened but cover all the necessary basics. Each firefighter will have the skills required to handle emergencies and react to other situations, a missing concept in many training programs. As a training officer, you should always ask yourself if your training program benefits the firefighters. It would be best if you critically analyzed it to avoid any bias. In many situations, you will find no answer, which is why fire department changes are needed.

Quality

Quality is crucial in designing, implementing, and tracking training data and information. We have learned these steps throughout these chapters, but we can always remind ourselves what they mean.

Designing

Designing is the actual making of training programs. A training officer should consider various aspects when designing a training program. For example, some of these aspects may include (but shouldn't be limited to) NFPA standards, mission needs, service delivery capabilities, firefighters' experience, and departments' standard operating procedures (or guidelines). It would be illogical for a training officer to formulate a training program with drills for new firefighters who have never stretched a line into a building, thrown a ladder, searched a smoke-filled or low-visibility room, etc. New firefighters have different needs from continuing firefighters. The plan becomes ineffective if the officer constructs a training program that mismatches these needs.

Implementing

The training officer should consider the department's budget when implementing a training program. It will make zero sense for a training program to have numerous drills requiring special props that they may not have available. A good training officer should formulate interventions for such situations and have the department network with others, allowing them to use their props during training. As a result, the training meets quality standards.

Tracking

Despite quality being essential in tracking training data and information, quality is also crucial. This phase is the only phase where quantity becomes essential. For example, a training officer can track their records if the requirement is to have a minimum of 80 quality training hours annually and a firefighter only has 10% of those hours. The difference in training hours is where quantity becomes essential. There are zero excuses for someone with only eight training hours annually. It will be impossible to argue that those hours were effective. As a result, remedial training becomes a viable option for such firefighters.

Quality and Information Delivery

A training officer's role is to ensure firefighters understand their information and act according to their instructions. It will be inefficient if a training officer trains about saws training, yet firefighters cannot exchange oil in a saw. The outcomes of the training decide whether information delivery was effective.

Here are a few ways in which information delivery can be ascertained:

- Drills
- Lessons learned
- Positives
- Eye-opening details

Drills

The best way for a training officer to know whether their training is quality is through drills. This situation will analyze the efficiency of firefighters in the field. For example, if the class was about saws, there should be drills where firefighters use the saws to cut open roofs for ventilation. Remember, drills are the last step of the crawl-walk-run methodology. If the firefighters practice hose evolutions in a large square foot building, then they should practice "deep-seated stretches" in both the crawl and walk phases. Once your team has practiced that skill in understanding the types of obstacles, and the correct hose length to choose, they should be ready to perform those skills in the run phase aka the drill. This will show that the training is designed to meet quality standards. If not, the training officer should consider repeating the crawl-walk-run methodology.

Lessons Learned

The lessons learned are what firefighters understand about the training. For example, if the training officer is training the basics of proper apparatus positioning, the takeaway should be that the firefighters understand the importance of proper apparatus positioning and also how each apparatus works. If they are driving and operating an engine, they should know the best position for effective hose deployment while leaving room for the ladder truck.

In the same case, if they are driving and operating an aerial apparatus *"truck, ladder, tower"* they should be able to have good familiarization and experience in the length of that apparatus, how long it is, if the bucket has an overhang off the back, how far the out-riggers come out (so they don't crush the cop car parked right in front of the address *lol*), overhead obstructions such as wires, trees, branches, etc. These specific items are the quality piece of the training sessions, this allows them to respond to emergencies effectively.

Positives

The training should have positives. The training officer should listen to the firefighters and know what they think about the training. In most cases, if the training hours are monotonous, it will be easy to tell from the look of the firefighters. Long training hours are a recipe for training negatives, which is why the training officer should ascertain that training hours be kept to a minimum.

Eye Opening Details

This element is arguably vital to learning whether firefighters understood their training. For example, if the training is on structural firefighting and firefighters respond by asking about concepts that the training officer never mentioned, it becomes apparent that the training was quality. Quality is not always about reducing the time meant for training programs. It demands that firefighters understand the concepts they are being caught. If not, the training becomes ineffective even if the training officer reduces the number of training hours.

Quality Training

We have learned about what quality means to the training program and the outcomes required from a quality program. We are now supposed to examine what a quality training program should have. These requirements are sadly unavailable in many fire departments for various reasons, including ignorance, budget issues, and leadership constraints. My experience as a training officer has taught me that a training program should include these elements to succeed.

Failing to have these elements is what breeds confusion and misunderstandings in training. These elements include:

- Service Delivery Capabilities (SDC)
- Mission needs
- Skillset of firefighters
- Needs of the firefighters

Service Delivery Capabilities (SDC)

We learned about this concept in the previous chapter. I explained to you that I divided these capabilities into four cores. The "Core-four" include:

- Structural firefighting
- Hazardous materials
- Emergency medical services
- Technical rescue

Each core had other disciplines. For example, structural firefighting had disciplines like pre-incident planning and driver training. Furthermore, each discipline had operational requirements, frequency, and METL. This explanation is what quality training is. As a training officer, you should first divide your SDC into cores from which you will develop other disciplines. Doing this action will allow you to save time and train firefighters on a specific concept rather than overall training.

Mission Needs

The mission of any fire department is to ensure that it provides community safety while ensuring that the safety requirements for firefighters and others in the fire department are met. This situation begs the question of what the fire department can do to improve safety requirements. The first step has a training program that matches these expectations. The main activity that happens in any fire department daily is training. Through it, firefighters can improve community safety while also improving their ability to proficiently operate in a safe manner.

It, therefore, makes zero sense if the training is tedious and non-informative. For example, if a training officer incorporates extremely long hours in their training, the chances of firefighters getting injured can be very high, especially if the training is non-stop. As a result, the training program fails to meet quality standards because it is non-compliant with the department's mission. Instead, the training should cover the right amount of time needed to gain an understanding and develop proficiency to perform in the field safely.

Another way of looking at this situation is through emergencies. Firefighters should always be ready to act when emergencies arise. Their efficiency is not just about them availing themselves in the field but how they use their equipment. The training program fails if a firefighter is in the field and does not know the basics, like connecting a hydrant to the engine. You may argue that the training program is effective, but it is not. We have learned that quality training programs allow instructional delivery through positives, lessons learned, and after-actions. The training officer can identify which firefighters are unprepared to go to the field if they know what outcomes to expect from the training program.

Test Your Understanding

You are the training officer of XYZ fire department. After training, you notice that there are firefighters who provide new knowledge based on the concepts they have learned. Others are very effective in drills, giving the lessons they have learned. On the other hand, some are unaware of any of these concepts and keep quiet instead. As the training officer, you are happy with the training program's overall contributions because it shows it meets the quality demands. You then authorize all the firefighters to be cleared to go into the field.

Is this a right or wrong call?

- Yes
- No

The answer is No. The training program can be of quality, but it requires the training officer to emphasize its quality. The training officer should have asked the firefighters who remained silent about the problem. In some situations, they may be shy despite understanding the training. In other cases, they may be unaware of what is happening in training. As a result, some of the newer firefighters may not be completely prepared for operating in the field because they were shy or "escaped the radar" during on-the-job training.

Skillset of Firefighters

The training program for firefighters and fire inspectors cannot be the same. These two individuals have different jobs, making their skillset different. If a fire department has the same training program for these two professionals, it reduces the quality of training. The same concept applies to other professionals like fire chiefs and lieutenants. The training officer should match the skills required for the training. For example, firefighters mainly deal with current events, including stopping a fire in a building.

On the other hand, fire inspectors typically deal with pre- and post-events. If a fire occurred in a building, the fire inspectors or investigators would come after the firefighters had stopped the fire. Their role will be to determine what caused the fire and issue recommendations to avoid this situation from reoccurring. The difference in roles between the firefighters and fire inspectors is apparent, so the training needs to be different. Firefighters need to be trained in structural firefighting, while fire inspectors need to be trained in investigation techniques and inspection procedures.

Needs of the Firefighters

A quality training program should encompass the needs of the firefighters. For example, a fire department may have senior and new firefighters. Senior firefighters require repetition training to help them remember what they have already learned. New firefighters need different actions, including certification, and on-the-job training. They should be allowed to ease into the training slowly before adjusting to the regular training with the senior firefighters.

Test Your Understanding

You are the training officer in XYZ fire department. You realize that the department has brought on some new firefighters, and you decide the best approach is to combine them with senior firefighters as you develop their training program. After a while, you realize the new firefighters are training well with the senior firefighters. You ignore developing a new training plan for the new firefighters.

Is this a good move?

- Yes
- No

No. It is a wrong move because new firefighters' needs differ from those of the senior firefighters. For example, the new firefighters may need to go to a fire academy, which is a different situation for senior firefighters. Furthermore, the certifications required by the new firefighters are different from senior firefighters. New firefighters may need more certifications because they are starting their firefighting journey. As a result, only mixing them with senior firefighters may breed inefficiency because they may only learn one method.

So be mindful of who is training with and mentoring your new people. Senior firefighters may want to learn saw training through drills because they have completed the crawl and walk phases. On the other hand, new firefighters may want the theoretical aspect first because they are just starting the crawl-walk-run methodology.

Quantity Training

Quantity training is usually inefficient, especially if a firefighter is unaware of how to react during emergencies. A firefighter with more than 120 training hours annually is not expected to be more efficient than those with fewer hours. In many situations, those with lesser hours are more effective because they learned what was necessary and avoided what was unnecessary. Moreover, quantity training does not incorporate the crawl-walk-run methodology in most cases. Incorporating this methodology means that the training is quality-driven, the opposite of what we discuss in this sub-section.

As a training officer, firefighters look to you to issue them with the best training methodology. Quantity training is effective when tracking training data and information. If one misses training consistently, quantity training can effectively identify such people. As a result, training officers should consider incorporating this approach during tracking training data and information. Any other activity included through quantity training may become inefficient because quality training covers most of the efficient training.

Summary

We have looked at quality and quantity training. At this point, we should know that quality training is the most efficient, which is why fire departments should incorporate it. Furthermore, we have established that quantity training effectively tracks training data and information. Because it has an advantage, you, as the training officer, should find an equilibrium where you can use both techniques to boost overall training. This situation allows you to comply with the NFPA standards, reducing legal complexities. It also raises the question of what training should look like to meet the legal, quality, and quantity standards.

What Training Should Be

It Should Have a Purpose

The training should protect the lives of people and firefighters, including company officers and chief officers. Training as a routine becomes ineffective because it fails to realize the commitment of those being trained. The training officer sets the tone for the training. If the training officer trains firefighters as a routine, they fail to be effective because they will treat the training as routine. As a result, the training fails to meet quality and regulatory standards.

It Should Make Sense

Training should be applicable in the field. For example, saw training will assist firefighters in responding to emergencies relating to ventilation or other obstacles. They will use their saw training to cut roofs to vent smoke or windowpanes to cut out an obstruction like bars so they can remove a victim. This situation, therefore, matches the quality standards expected in every training.

People Doing Their Assignments Correctly

Training should provide the knowledge required for firefighters to perform their tactical duties. If they cannot perform their duties, like properly deploying hose lines in the field, they are doing their assignments incorrectly. This incorrect approach is because they do not understand the training. In such situations, the training officer should go back to the drawing board and establish ways to make the training effective for the firefighters.

Emergency Responsiveness

The more firefighters respond effectively to emergencies, the more effective the training. It indicates that the training is fulfilling its agenda of promoting public safety while also ensuring protection for those providing safety. Emergency responsiveness involves how well firefighters can handle an emergency in the field. The more they can exercise accuracy and calmly while performing their duties, the more it paints a positive image for the training.

Training Evolutions

Because training requirements are always changing, the training officer should incorporate these changes to make their training up-to-date. Do not be that training officer who ignores these changes because of your pride. I agree that some changes are redundant, but also, there are those which may be crucial. For example, real estate is an evolving field, meaning house designs are changing. The new designs are concepts firefighters should learn to make effective during emergencies. If the training officer refuses to incorporate such changes, you are putting the lives of the firefighters and the public at great risk. You should set aside your ego and do what is right to ensure that you promote the public and firefighters' safety.

Another example is the fast-rising business of Lithium/ION battery powered vehicles and other household items. The more these things become the "norm" the more risk we inherit to responding to an emergency involving these things. If we simply watched a quick "training" video online and filled out a training report stating that we attended lithium/ION emergency training. Did we really learn anything, or better yet... are we prepared to mitigate that type of emergency? The answer is no. This is the importance of quality training, we need to get real facts, and up the frequency to that types of training so we are better prepared.

High-Risk Vs. Low Frequency

The duties performed by firefighters are usually of high risk but low frequency. For example, building explosions are not daily occurrences but pose an increased risk regarding property damage, many injuries, and deaths. As a result, when analyzing the performance of fire departments, one should not look at how often they save people's lives but how they reduce the intensity of a given situation.

Unfortunately, fire departments face the issue of budget committees undervaluing their work by implementing budget cuts, especially if they do not exaggerate the frequency. It is a sad situation that many fire departments find themselves and one which requires immediate intervention.

Gordon Graham, a retired California State Police Highway Patrol veteran, teaches all over the United States (US) about high-risk vs. low frequency. He establishes that many emergency responders are fixated on frequency of emergencies and less on the preparation of responding to and mitigating those emergencies. Furthermore, many fire departments believe that stating unrealistic frequencies is the only way to get higher funding. For example, if a fire department stopped ten building fires in one year, the department may exaggerate and quote twenty. As a result, they expect the budget committee to provide more funding because they have stated a higher frequency.

Instead of going down this route, it is more sustainable if budget committees understand that firefighting is a high-risk, low-frequency job. As a result, their judgment should not be on the number of fires they put out but on ensuring that the firefighters are equipped and operationally proficient to mitigate most if not all types of potential emergencies, regardless of their frequency. More people will understand and appreciate the fire department's value through this approach.

In this same regard, quality training is important because your department may not have a high frequency of specific emergency responses. That is where the value of good quality training proves its weight in gold. That proficiency is gained through proper training, which ensures the level of readiness is there if ever called to those low frequency emergencies.

Training officers should understand the value of quality training. Quantity training fails to target the training's purpose, which is to ensure public safety and safety for those who are training. The training officer should focus on providing high-frequency training. This situation means they should do repetitive training to ensure firefighters know how to respond to emergencies. For example, some emergencies may require different types of skills needed to be performed during drills. Therefore, drills should not always practice the same set of skills and instead be different in their approach and design to ensure that firefighters reap the most benefits.

Program Designing Based on Quality

We described that quality training involves the incorporation of four components:

- Service Delivery Capabilities (SDC)
- Mission needs
- Skillset of firefighters
- Need of the firefighters

The training program should ensure it matches these requirements for it to be termed as quality. This situation makes training officers have their cores formulated from the SDC. It is the basic foundation from which training officers can ensure quality training.

Risk Exposing and Mitigation

The risk associated with the fire department is usually high. For example, fire departments may respond to a structural collapse emergency. Training officers should mitigate these risks by ensuring repetitive training. Repetition training allows firefighters to remind themselves of the basics through drills. As a result, they will always be ready to tackle these adverse situations.

Another point that training officers should know is that the low frequency of adverse situations does not guarantee few training sessions. Training officers should always treat these low-frequency events as high-frequency because it will mean that they train more on the issue. For example, they may instill more structural firefighting drills to prepare firefighters.

Test Your Understanding

Assume you are the training officer of *XYZ* fire department. You analyze the number of emergencies you have handled over the year and notice that there are not as many as you thought. Furthermore, structure fires only happened ten times that calendar year. As a result, you reduce the structural drills for that training. In your head, you imagine that you are saving the fire department money by not having those types of firefighting drills.

Are you providing quality training?

- Yes
- No

No. Despite quality training demanding that training should not focus on training hours, it is your duty as the training officer to issue the required training to firefighters. You should understand that firefighting is a high-risk, low-frequency job, so firefighters should always be ready to react to an emergency. Getting them ready demands having high-frequency training on the low-frequency event. Repetition training allows them to gather the knowledge and expertise required to tackle this high-risk situation.

Know Your Mission

As stated earlier, a fire department's mission is to ensure public safety and safety for those it trains. As a result, all training should be focused on achieving this situation. For example, the training should issue the firefighters with the knowledge required to negate an adverse situation. In keeping the public safe, the firefighters also protect their lives because their training allows them to do so.

Know Your Response Area

Get out and learn your response area. Is there "down-time" during certain days or seasons? Of course, there is! Even the busiest fire stations in the world have "down-time". Take advantage of that time and go drive around your response area. Learn run-routes, practice apparatus positioning, etc. While driving around, you may discover or refamiliarize yourself with areas of special interest within your response area. Special interest (or special hazards) may include chemical plants, senior citizens homes, industrial warehouses, shopping malls, schools, etc. Realizing such aspects lets you know which areas are the most susceptible to high-risk calamities. As a result, you will always be ready to tackle such areas because training focuses on guaranteeing safety within these areas.

Summary

My experience as a training officer lets me know why quality training is essential. I also apply this concept in my leadership program. I ensure the program is not more than four hours because this time is sufficient to get the experience and engagement, I want with those I am teaching. This situation is not to say that if you teach more than four, then it is inefficient. It is my personal experience and is why I am not keen on the number of training hours a firefighter completes. Instead, I am interested in the knowledge and networks they have developed because of the training.

A VIEW FROM EXPERIENCE

By: Conor Miller
Lieutenant, West Point (NY) Fire Department

Conor Miller has been with the West Point Fire Dept for over 15 years and is currently serving as a Lieutenant on Engine 1/Rescue 1. He holds experience with both volunteer and career fire departments and technical rescue teams. He teaches for NYS OFPC's special operations branch and Orange County NY's Fire training center. He is currently the Training Officer for the Orange County Technical Rescue Team's Rope Division.

There is no silver bullet when it comes to perfecting your training plan or style. What works for one department most certainly won't be a perfect fit for another. A dedicated engine company, with no other disciplines or assignments, gets to focus on the singular task of putting water on fire. Their plan can break down and perfect each piece of engine company operations and the perfection of their craft. However, in today's all hazard fire service, finding a crew that doesn't perform multiple disciplines is next to impossible. As we begin to add hazmat, Emergency Medical, technical services and any other tasks that have been asked of the fire service as the years go on how do we continue to perfect our craft? We should focus on optimizing our time on the training ground and make all of our second's count. Our job as leaders is to determine the quality and quantity needed for training.

We should set our priorities early and reevaluate our purpose within the community of which we serve before we can figure out how our training plan needs to work. Most of this is going to fall on chief officers, but it's equally important for company officers and firefighters as well as it is usually them delivering the training. We can't forget our primary purpose, our identity, and our promise to the community, we are a fire department. No other service or agency is expected to show up when someone's house is on fire. As our fire prevention services and building codes continue to show great success our working fires continue to drop. This is great, but we have to remember that just because they happen less often, doesn't mean they are any less important. When there is a fire, we show up, that was the deal when all of us took the oath.

With fire suppression at the top of our list we should be conducting our own no fluff risk assessment to figure out what our community needs from us. All too often departments get bogged down providing services for which their community has no use for. If you have no water in or around your district, then it is probably reasonable not to spend any hour's training on dive rescue. No mountains or tall buildings, then you probably don't need to have a rope team.

If the company one district over runs a heavy rescue dedicated to technical services, should we be spending training hours in our engine company on structural collapse? Every department has their own circumstances, but it's up to us to make sure that we are doing what is best to provide for our community but also making sure our firefighters are ready, proficient, and safe.

After we figure out what to train on, we have to figure out how much of it we need. Today's fire service is rife with metrics. And in 2023 that is a necessary evil. As much as most of us wish for more jobs and less paperwork, the reality is the scales don't side in our favor. Reporting software has become the key to justifying budgets, applying for grants, tracking training, and a litany of other administrative duties. Because of this, we tend to think of our training as a series of hours, instead of tasks. Training such as continuing education hours for EMS, decontamination procedures for hazmat and hose line advancement for structural firefighting are recorded in neat blocks of time between the hours of this and that. The drill ground can sometimes garner the feel of a time clock that you should punch in and punch out. Our job as leaders and instructors is to understand the importance of the metrics required to keep the department running while not letting training feel like a shift at the factory where we watch the clock. The quality of our training needs to surpass the quantity of time we decide to track.

One of the biggest tightropes we should walk when administering quality training is in its level of complexity. If your goal for every drill is to make it as simple as possible and provide little to no real-world hazards, then you are doing a severe disservice to both you and your crew. If every class you teach, you drive your students into the ground, then you are making no friends and losing the students interest in the topic you are teaching. We have to find a balance. Small company drills after a run, or on the way back from the gym can be thinking and discussion-type learning. It's a great opportunity to assess the level of understanding of the people you work with and to let newer instructors have the opportunity to lead. But if we pull a company to the training ground for the sole intention of doing firefighter rescue, then we should be doing firefighter rescues as close to real as we can make it. It is my sincere hope I never respond to a fire harder than some of the training I've participated in. I owe it to my crew to provide them with the same level of training.

Good training doesn't have to be long. If you're practicing something full speed, like a difficult hose stretch, what is the reasonable time you would expect it to take a fully trained crew? Maybe 10 minutes from start to finish? Ask yourself, did they accomplish what we came to do? Drills like this are real and valuable and don't need to take all afternoon. My experience with real drills, run full speed, is the buy-in of the members usually takes the drill beyond the basic parameters you set for it. People enjoy doing this job and working through the challenges it presents. If we foster and encourage that you'll find members wanting to push the drill past its original goal. They'll ask questions like "What if we tried this instead?" or "Did you see the video where this happened?". Task-oriented training allows for companies to stay proficient and engaged while the drills stay short and practical.

While we start to initiate task-based training, we have to be wary of "checking the box." We usually use the term checking the box to describe something we all have to do, but don't want to do or agree with. Nobody wants to do their annual online training that human resources requires but we do it because we have to. We want to assure we are generating a training environment that doesn't have the crews thinking "let's go check this box and get it over with." The first step to this is keeping the training practical and applicable. Throwing a wrench in during training evolutions has its value, but you will quickly lose buy in if every scenario you set up has crazy stipulations. The best way to keep members involved is to include them and to value their input when it's provided. Ask "what do you guys want to work on?" and let members who speak up with constructive advice or input say what they want to say. You have to have a certain amount of self-confidence to run any sort of training program, and nothing displays that more than allowing others to share their opinions and knowledge without discounting it to make yourself look better.

When we look at the people, we are training our goal is for all of them to be outstanding in what they do. The quality of the training we provide will show this in time. We have to understand what level of outstanding we can expect from each individual that is participating. Some people are going to need repetition of skills for tasks that others pick up quickly. Sometimes that depends on the person, other times it depends on the task. Our job is to make sure we don't discredit anyone who is actually trying and learning, even if they aren't doing it on our timetable. I have taught people who required something to be reviewed ten different times in ten different ways, however now they can perform that skill marginally better than the student who picked it up first time with little explanation. We set the stage for a quality training environment and that stage needs to include the fostering off all types of learning abilities and personalities.

Practicality is key in controlling both our quality and quantity of training. We have already discussed our risk assessment and how we need to determine what training we should be doing. Next, we need to find the most efficient way to get there. The basic template of "crawl, walk, run" works great but we tend to stray away from it quickly. We can't expect someone to complete a task if they don't understand it, so we start at a crawl. Then we practice it working through the kinks in the walk stage until finally we are ready to run it full speed with real world hazards and simulations. Unfortunately, we often make one of two mistakes. We either start at run or stop at walk. When we run all task-oriented training at full speed we often leave behind those who don't fully understand the concepts or skills were trying to teach. Conversely if we start at crawl and don't move past the walk stage then we never actually mastered the skill we were hoping to learn. Don't be afraid to start over and slow the training down for newer and senior members alike, dusting up on the basics of why we do a task is always valuable. But we have to assure we work towards the mastery of performing the skill how we will in real life scenarios if we want our training to count for anything.

While we work to keep our training practical it's important that we focus on keeping it efficient. Lately there seems to be a large push on social platforms to try to accomplish our training tasks by treating them like games. Ideas like practicing air consumption through a game of dodgeball or vehicle extrication with a game of Jenga are wasted movements. If you want to practice air consumption, practice a fireground task that will require us to use air. Moving a 2.5" hose line will use plenty of air with the added benefit of also practicing moving a hose line. These creative games have been introduced to increase buy in by members at training events. My experience is the best buy in is created by doing real training that includes the input and participation of the firefighters who joined to perform the duties of a firefighter.

Our training and PPE are the only thing that set us apart from civilians at the scene of an emergency. Once we are provided with the proper gear and equipment it's up to us as leaders in the fire service to provide the training that will truly make a difference when the bell rings. When it comes to quantity, we have to ensure we are training on the right topics for our community. We should document accordingly to assure our firefighters are properly represented and receive what they need. And we have to ensure we're performing training on a continuous basis. None of that truly matters, however, if we don't emphasize quality in everything we do. Quality in the way we approach our training tasks, and, in the focus, we put into getting the most out of the training we provide. And quality in the way we treat our students and coworkers to assure we are at our best to provide the service people expect from us. When we get stuck in the rut of laziness or lackluster training, we have to hold ourselves accountable.

We need to remember the people who depend on us. Our community, our families, our fellow firefighters expect the best and the most positive outcomes. If our training isn't set up to provide that for them, we need to course correct to meet their expectations. Expectations that we should all be working toward regardless of rank or time on the job.

Chapter 10

Having What It Takes

My general life experience has taught me the significance of being an inspiration to others, which I believe has assisted me in becoming a successful training officer. There are qualities that a training officer should possess to be effective in the development of firefighters. I have my top ten traits that I believe each training officer should have. I learned these traits through my journey to becoming a good training officer. I have always had to earn anything through my efforts. Through my career as a firefighter, training was not always offered to me. In most cases I found myself using my own time and dime in an effort to attend certification level courses.

Dependence was not something I incorporated in my younger life stages. For example, I paid for my hotels each time I had to travel to take a class, which kept changing because classes were in different parts of the US such as Alabama, New York, Maryland, West Virginia, Indiana as well as different cities in New Jersey and Pennsylvania. By paying for these classes with my own money and using my accrued vacation leave, this denied me time with my family, including my wife and children. Studying kept me from my family and took a large quantity of my vacation leave, but it was unavoidable because I had to gather knowledge and specific certifications in an effort to develop my education and experience and market myself for my future aspirations of leading my own teams and programs one day.

Education is important because it offers us the ability to reference things as we grow into our careers. Knowledge and training help us have a clear vision of how to design and develop more efficient programs that help build our firefighters. Knowledge and training help us be more prepared for what is to come and helps solidify our professional assessment on matters due to our background in the subject or situation.

So as a training officer, you should ask yourself the following question: Do you have what it takes? Regardless of your answer, look at my top ten for a training officer and see if they match yours. If you don't have your own top ten, here are mine, my hope is you learn from them and incorporate them, and I assure you that you will be a great training officer.

1. Be a student
2. Be an educator
3. Be an inspiration
4. Be credible
5. Be a leader
6. Be confident
7. Be humble
8. Be resourceful
9. Be passionate
10. Leave a good legacy

1. Be a Student

Just because you are a training officer, does not mean you should stop attending classes or earning certifications. You should be ready to accept that just because you are the training officer, does not mean you are always the subject matter expert. However, because of your responsibility as the training officer, it is worth arguing that you should continue to learn as much as possible. The fire service is ever evolving, and due to that fact, you should make an effort to be as prepared and educated as you can. The question becomes what you should do to better your craft. Taking more classes to earn knowledge will be an essential step to others appreciating and respecting you. Knowledge is limitless, and no one has 100% knowledge of everything. This situation, therefore, means that there is always an opportunity for you to learn if you are ready.

For example, recently Lithium-Ion battery emergencies have increased. As the training officer, it should be a priority for you to gain as much information and knowledge about how to prepare your people to respond to this new type of emergency. Do not let your ego get the best of you and decide to ignore these updates because you think you know everything. Instead, accept that you are still a student and master your craft. How many people in society in their forties are still in school? Over 1.6 million people in the U.S. are enrolled in college that are above the age of forty. The point here is to never stop learning! Knowledge is powerful; the more you have it, the more prepared you are to respond to situations. Therefore, remain a student and develop your craft.

The main advantage of being a student is that your instruction delivery will improve massively. You can see things from a bird's eye view (360 degrees). We learned about the bird's eye view in chapter 4, and we mentioned how significant it is for a training officer to see things this way. You can only see things wholly if you remain a student. Being a student demands that you stay open to new ideas and not be too rigid.

Test Your Understanding

You are the training officer of XYZ fire department. One of your firefighters comes up with a better way of handling training and decides to tell you in private. You see the idea and accept in your mind that it is a good idea. Instead of trying to see how you could implement the idea, you criticize the firefighter for attempting to intimidate you. The firefighter tells you they did not mean any harm, which is why they searched for you in private. You refuse to listen and dismiss them.

Is the training officer right in his actions?

- Yes
- No

The answer is No. A training officer who was open-minded would have paid more attention and listened to what the firefighter was proposing. Furthermore, because the firefighter searched for you in person and privately, the firefighter respected you. The best you can do to earn more respect is to listen to the idea and see how you could implement it. Refusing the idea and throwing unnecessary shade at the firefighter shows how insecure you are as a training officer. This trait does not show any act of being a student of the craft.

Things you should incorporate to be a successful student of the craft include:

- Be open-minded
- Seek more knowledge by attending more classes
- Listen to other people's views even if they are regardless of rank or seniority, any information is good information.

As a result, you will reap benefits like:

- Seeing things from a bird's eye view (360 degrees)
- You will be more prepared
- Your peers and the firefighters will respect you more

2. Be an Educator

As a training officer, firefighters depend on you for knowledge and expertise. They expect you to teach them how to be better in their jobs because it makes them safe in the field. Furthermore, it makes them achieve the fire department's primary mission, ensuring public safety. If you are a poor educator, you risk the lives of the firefighters and the public. Your aim should always be to ensure that firefighters are better than you. If they become better than you, you are doing your job correctly.

If you are a training officer afraid of firefighters surpassing your ability and expertise, then you do not deserve the responsibility of developing others. As a training officer, you are a leader, and it should always be in your best interest to ensure that you prepare others to make them more successful.

Have a Good Understanding of Psychology

A training officer should know when to be empathetic, sympathetic, and strict. There are times when firefighters may be going through fatigue and burnout and overworking them just because you want to disseminate knowledge is inappropriate. Instead, as a good educator, you should be sympathetic and empathetic in such a situation and encourage them that things will improve.

Encourage Others to Be at Their Best

Everybody has different abilities. This situation also applies to the fire department. As the training officer, you should not force everyone to be as successful as the "best" firefighter. The truth is, in some cases, it is impossible.

What you should do is encourage them to be better versions of themselves. Repeatedly doing this action shows how good you are as an educator, and more firefighters will feel comfortable around you. It is the training officer's responsibility to develop the future leaders of the fire service. It is high time the training officers stop holding their people back and start building their people to be ready to receive the torch when it is ready to be passed.

Understand the Significance of the Fire Department's Mission

As training officer, you know how vital your mission is in preparing yourself to become a better educator. This situation is because you understand how detrimental it will be if you fail to incorporate better training standards. The safety of the public and our firefighters' safety should always be your number one priority, and you will strive to ensure that each firefighter improves their skillset. The other benefit is that you will not tolerate complacency, demanding firefighters be ready for their training. This situation is where quantitative training will be efficient. A good educator will examine the training sessions attended by their firefighters. If these sessions are unsatisfactory, you will apply the necessary interventions, including remedial training.

3. Be an Inspiration

What is inspiration? Do you inspire others? Do others see you as a mentor or an ordinary training officer? These are some of the questions you should ask yourself as a training officer to determine whether you inspire others.

Firefighters become Better Versions of Themselves

When you inspire firefighters, they will automatically want to make you proud. Furthermore, they will want to see themselves overachieving because they know their training officer believes in them. As a result, they perform better, which then offers better public safety.

Better Teams Make a Better Workplace

Imagine a fire department that was full of conflicts; what would be the first things that come to mind? Poor training and inadequate leadership. Good leadership involves being a good source of inspiration. You cannot be a good leader without inspiring others. If you fail at inspiring others to build cohesion throughout the workforce, then the firefighters within your organization stand the risk of poor performance. They would also be subject to injury due to their inadequate training program. That inadequate training program is a product of your inability to inspire others and build a team. The firefighters will not take training seriously nor have a level of mutual trust with you or one another because training is simply a chore and not for professional development.

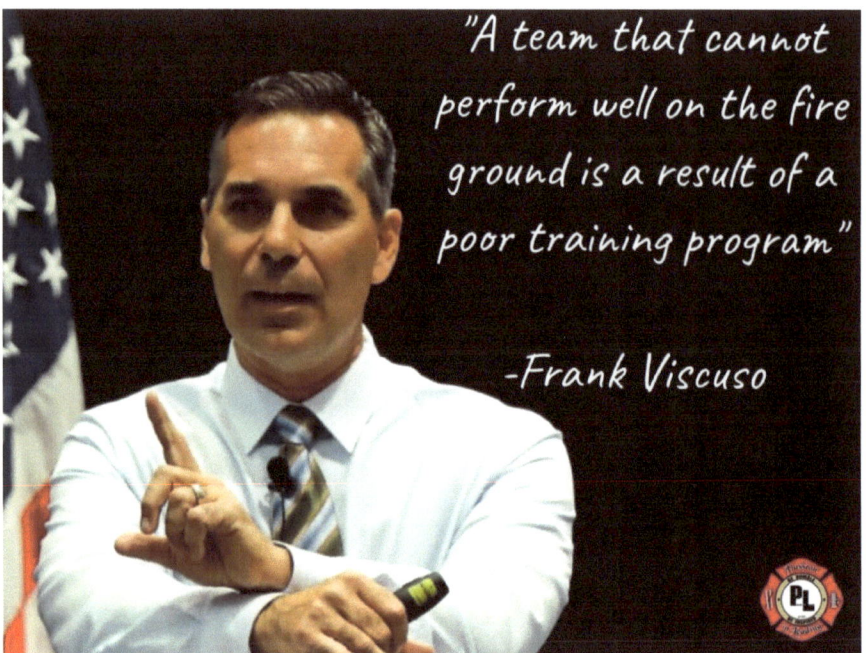

Sources of Inspiration

As a training officer, you should ask yourself how to be a better inspirator. Some good inspiration sources include:

- Historic Leaders
- Fire department's veterans
- Athletes
- Books about leadership and motivation
- Past and Present Fire Instructors
- Coaches
- Teachers (Educators)
- Mentors
- Training Conferences (FDIC International)
- Personal/Professional Development workshops (symposiums)

4. Be Credible

Credibility is essential in the fire department. Growing up in New Jersey there was a saying for those who were fake, *"Fugazi"* which is a term I have used throughout my career and in my lectures when I describe a training officer who is simply faking it until they make it. A training officer should be credible to make others respect and listen to them. You should have the experience needed to teach firefighters. It is illogical for you, the training officer, to demand others to listen to you when you have never been in the field. It is impractical. If you wanted firefighters to listen to you, you should have gathered the experience needed when you were a firefighter.

Basic skills that a training officer should have experience in are:

- Searching a smoke-filled structure
- Drive/Operate an Engine or Ladder Truck
- Talk responsibly on the radio
- Experience in leadership

These skills automatically show the firefighters that you are proficient in what you do, and they can depend on you for training. Someone who knows nothing of these actions will find it challenging to train firefighters because you have no idea what you are actually talking about. If you are not proficient in these actions, you will lose respect from your firefighters, which you may see as insubordinate, but it is within their right to do so, because due to your inexperience, they have no reason to have faith in you to develop them, thus eroding the much-needed mutual trust. Remember, the training officer should be an educator. How do you become a good educator? Simple, be credible! And how do you be credible? Value your experience and knowledge.

Test Your Understanding

You are the training officer of *XYZ* fire department. You know you have zero field experience because you have been at the desk all your professional life. Because your relative was the fire chief of *XYZ* fire department, they pulled some strings to fit you in the training officer's position. You know you do not deserve this position based on your field experience, but you tell yourself that you are the right person for the job. Your first few weeks assigned to training, your instruction to the firefighters went well, but now it is time for them to start doing practical activities. The next training is saws training, and they ask you how it feels while using a "K12" to cut window bars during emergencies. You remain silent because you lack the answer to give them.

Firefighters start talking about your field inexperience, and you take it personally. You punish them by making them do extra training sessions, telling them they are crucial to them. One of the firefighters speaks out in anger and says sarcastically, "What do you know about field experience?"

Is the firefighter right to ask this statement?

In this context, the firefighter is within their rights to ask this question. The firefighter understands the cruel nature of the job because it may lead to death if a poor training officer is given to them. As a result, the firefighter asks the training officer about their experience because the training officer is not credible enough to teach the firefighters.

This situation shows that fire chiefs and other fire heads should be vigilant in who they employ as a training officer. This position is the fire department's vital position because it shows whether it complies with its mission. If a credible training officer is given to the firefighters, the chances of producing skilled firefighters are high.

Therefore, as a training officer, ask yourself this question; are you credible? If you are not, the best thing to do is seek another position or as harsh as it sounds, just leave the fire service. Simply put, all of those years of you going to the back of the line to escape being exposed for your deficiencies in tactical performance coupled with every day you remain in the office, proves you are not credible and that my friend puts the lives of many firefighters and society at risk.

5. Be a Leader

We discussed the essence of leadership in a training officer. As the training officer, firefighters look up to you for guidance. They expect you to be their role model because you have more significant experience in firefighting. You are required to lead them because it is your duty. To be a good leader, you need to provide firefighters with a good training program, know what is at stake, and take responsibility for firefighters' actions.

Develop a Good Training Program

One of the best ways a training officer can show leadership traits is by constructing an efficient training program. This program determines the effectiveness of any training, and as the leader, you should demand a specific level of output from each firefighter. Being strict on how training is done makes you lead from the front because it shows you value the firefighters' safety.

Know What's at Stake

A good leader always knows the ramifications of not doing things correctly. The training officer should understand that if training is done poorly, the public and firefighters' safety is jeopardized. As a result, you should always demand 100% from your firefighters to ensure they adhere to the organization's mission.

Take Responsibility for Firefighters' Actions

A good leader takes responsibility for their subordinates' actions. You train the firefighters, making you responsible for their actions if they do as you instructed them. If you let your ego blind you and refuse to take responsibility for your actions, you become the problem within your organization and productivity will slow down resulting in a regression in the skillset.

6. Be Confident

As a training officer, you should be confident in what you know and your delivery when instructing. You handle the training of many firefighters, requiring a confident individual. If you are a person who is shaky when training firefighters, it makes you look weak. Some firefighters may see you as unreliable because you are shy, yet you have massive field experience and all the relevant certifications.

Always remember that confidence is more of a psychological thing than physical. If you tell yourself, "I've got this", you will offer a significant level of professional instruction. Furthermore, it would be best if you refused to get intimidated because it undermines your confidence. Remember refusing to get intimidated does not mean that you become rude. You can be confident and reject intimidation, but still remain professional.

Remember that you gain more confidence if you have the following things:

- Field experience
- Relevant certifications
- Ability to receive criticism
- A student of the craft
- A good leader
- Have no ego

These six things will prepare you to learn; therefore, you will remain unshaken if or when someone challenges you. Instead, if you have an ego and believe everyone should listen to you because it is your right, you will find it hard to remain confident during challenging times. As a result, you will be exposed as a training officer lacking in one of the essential traits of leadership.

7. Be Humble

Being humble does not mean allowing others to walk over you and remain silent. It enables you to know when to stay quiet and when to act. The training officer should be humble because it allows them to appreciate the firefighters' efforts. If you are a training officer and never appreciate your firefighters' work, this section should serve as a wake-up call that you need to exercise humility.

Being humble allows others to respect you, giving you a more significant following. Firefighters will know they can count on you to be there for them. as a training officer, my door is always open for all firefighters if they need assistance professionally or want to talk about their struggles. My firefighters know I will be there for them, so they are free to tell me anything that bothers them. I would not have attained this relationship with my firefighters if I had been arrogant. Instead, my humility allowed me to have better relationships with my firefighters, allowing them to be more productive in their training.

This situation goes to show why all training officers should be humble. It allows us to instruct firefighters because they are willing to listen. If you are an arrogant training officer, the chances of firefighters listening to you are very low. What ends up happening is that firefighters will not be ready for the field, leading to public safety concerns and more injuries to firefighters. Therefore, you should be prepared to be humble as a training officer to stand any chance of being listened to by the firefighters.

8. Be Resourceful

Resourcefulness means how efficient you are in solving problems. Problem-solving is a mandatory skill for all training officers. You should understand that society's cost of living is very high, which leads to budget cuts. These cuts affect training because there may be inadequate money to make props. As the cost-of-living increases, the cost of wood and fuel also increases, meaning that fire departments have to spend more on wood to make their props. This situation develops a significant problem: How can the training officer guarantee effective training? The answer is simple, be resourceful.

And how do you be resourceful? By networking. Remember what we discussed in chapter 7: networking begins with a handshake and a smile. You should develop networks with other fire departments because you can then share training sessions, allowing you not to feel the effects of budget cuts. In other situations, you can network with real estate developers to get the schematics of new house designs and incorporate them into training.

Being resourceful ensures you make the best out of a worse situation. If you want your training to be more sensitive to the department's locality, you should contact real estate developers or the city council to give you a list of special-hazard or high-hazard building types within your first-due area. The list may include chemical plants, which allow you to train your firefighters on handling an emergency related to a hazardous materials response, or could include senior citizen (assisting living), as well as child daycare facilities and the list goes on. This training would be impossible if you were not resourceful and got the required schematics for the region. By being resourceful you help yourself find new and meaningful methods to secure cost-effective training when facing potential budget

Test Your Understanding

You are the training officer of XYZ fire department. The department has experienced a massive budget cut, so training will not be the same. Furthermore, the department cannot support potential costs endured by training. You start complaining about this situation in front of firefighters and telling them their safety is at risk. You insist that if the situation is not corrected, they may pay the price through injuries and, in some instances, death.

Are you right in making these accusations?

Despite the statements being true, a resourceful training officer should not complain in front of the firefighters. You are not helping them by complaining in front of them. Instead, what you should do is find solutions. You are the training officer, and part of your responsibility is formulating the best situation out of a complicated one.

Instead of complaining, you can start networking with other training officers from different fire departments and develop a strategy that will allow you to train together. It would help to target the fire departments within your locality because training together makes sense. After all, you will be more proactive during emergencies.

Furthermore, maintaining a calm mind in such incidents makes firefighters respect you. If you complain about these issues in front of them, you make them disrespect you because they see you as an ineffective leader. If you have to raise your frustrations, look for the fire chief and discuss with them, the challenges training will likely face because of the reduced funding. If not, be smart and innovative, and search for ways that training can be effective with reduced funding.

9. Be Passionate

As a training officer, you should love what you do. The firefighting experience is not for anyone; those who chose this path did it because they are passionate about the job. If you are a training officer and you always complain about how tough the job is, you should quit because the chances of you training firefighters well are minimal. On the other hand, if you are passionate about your job, you will be determined to ensure that all firefighters receive the best training, allowing them to be successful in their duties to ensure public safety. As a result, passionate training officers are essential in ensuring they inspire others, creating room for future effective training officers.

You will accrue numerous benefits for being passionate about your training officer duties. They include:

- You will be resourceful
- You will remain open-minded
- You will always be ready to learn, meaning that you will remain a student of the craft
- The chances of firefighters respecting you will be higher
- You will inspire others
- You will leave a good legacy

I believe that these outcomes are what all training officers desire to achieve because it paints a good image. Well, you can achieve them by being passionate about your job. Your passion will drive you to achieve other positive outcomes that you may not have known. So, what is stopping you from being passionate about your training officer duties?

10. Leave A Good Legacy

When it comes to leaving a good legacy, the best quote to describe it is: "leave it better than how you found it." This quote in this context means that a training officer should focus their actions on ensuring that all firefighters are not the same after training. The target should always be to ensure that they have learned something new to make them ready to tackle various situations. The whole idea is to ensure that you inspire others to do great. You should ensure that they go beyond what they thought they could do. Consistently doing this will ensure that they remember you as someone who made them excellent firefighters.

Have you ever heard someone quoting their training officers like they do great generals or leaders? Not so much. This situation bothers me because a good training officer should be the one who served justly in a position of influence with the priority focus of developing others.

This situation is not the case because many training officers do not leave a good legacy. People remember you for the impact you had on their life. You will have a good legacy if you develop good firefighters and allow them to reach their potential.

My hope is that I am on my journey to leaving a good legacy. I always encourage my firefighters to be the best version of themselves both in the fire service and in life. I will not formulate regulations because they would fit my agenda but because I want them to work for the firefighters. Without looking after their best interests, I would fail as a training officer and would certainly leave a poor legacy. Instead, I try to be more inclusive in leading and training them. Where will you celebrate your retirement party when you leave? In a phone booth? How many people are going to attend your party? Just you! Answering these questions should help you evaluate what type of training officer you are.

Being a training officer is a high honor and should be taken as a privilege and not as a steppingstone. You are in a position of influence and should be playing a key role in the professional development of your people. Be their mentor, be their coach, be their leader, and be an inspiration! Establish an environment that warrants the very best from people, one that displays comfort and stability. Seek improvement in yourself while seeking improvement in the program that you are responsible for. You may be the person who helped develop the next great firefighter or chief officer. The one that they quote and write books about. That's how important your responsibility is, take it seriously, have what it takes!

Be the Training Officer that you wanted when you were them. Train them to be better than they were yesterday!

All my best in your future as you not only develop others, but also develop yourself.

Having What It Takes: The Training Officer's Top Ten

> ### A VIEW FROM EXPERIENCE
>
> By: Frank Viscuso
> Deputy Chief (ret.), Kearny (NJ) Fire Department
>
> Frank Viscuso is a retired deputy fire chief and the best-selling author of eight books on leadership, team development and customer service. He is an international speaker who travels throughout the world providing leadership training to various teams and industries including the emergency services, professional athletics, sales teams, the healthcare industry, small businesses, and large corporations. His popular keynotes, seminars and books are designed to introduce people to the skills needed to lead, inspire, and motivate their teams.

I did not set out to become my department's training officer. In fact, when the training officer in my department was getting promoted, he spent the next few weeks, asking every other officer on our department the same questions, "Are you interested in becoming our next training officer?" As expected, most of the officers answered with the same two letter answer, "NO."

When he came around to me, I asked, "What does a training officer do?"

During our short conversation, he talked about the duties and skills needed for that position. I didn't feel that I had the writing, presentation, and organization skills he spoke about, so I replied with, "Thank you for asking, but I don't think it's for me."

The following day, I was brought into the Chiefs officer where he congratulated me on being the new training officer of our organization. My eyes widened as I replied with, "ME? Why Me?"

To which he answered, "You showed the most interest."

If you have ever heard my story, then you know this ended up being the best thing that could have ever happened to me and my career from a professional standpoint. The challenge I had came early on in the process when I had to figure everything out as if I was the first person to ever be assigned as a department training officer. There was little guidance, and no mentorship provided. It was just, sign here kid… now go do something.

After developing more than 50 Standard operating guidelines, acquiring vacant buildings for training, bringing in millions in grant money, developing a probationary firefighter and driver training program, and eventually writing 8 best-selling fire service books, I can honestly say that none of this would have happened without being assigned to that position. Looking back, after reading this chapter, the only thing I wish I had was Dave's list. **Be a student, an educator, an inspiration, credible, confident, humble, resourceful, passionate**, and most of all, **be a good leader**, which will ensure you **leave a good legacy**.

Understand that you do not have to have it all figured out. Set goals, establish a game plan, and take action with specific intent. You can make a positive impact in your organization and do what you are meant to do… leave it better than you found it.

Frank Viscuso

Author of *Step Up and Lead*.

Appendix A
Suggested Training Requirements

SUGGESTED TRAINING REQUIRMENTS PER POSITION

FIREFIGHTER

METL	FREQUENCY
Fire Officer Development	
Leadership Training	Semi-Annual
Emergency Medical Technician	
Emergency Medical Technician (Continuing Education)	Monthly
CPR	Bi-Annual
Operational Requirements	
Structural Firefighting	Monthly
Pre-Incident Planning	Monthly
Drivers Training	Quarterly
Hazardous Materials	Quarterly
Technical Rescue	Quarterly
Pump Operations	Quarterly
Motor Vehicle Extrication	Annually
Breathing Apparatus	Annually
Fire Department Communications	Annually
Wildland Firefighting	Annually
Vehicle/Industrial Rescue	Annually
Fire Inspection Procedures	Annually
Building Construction	Annually
Specific Hazardous Processes/Permits	Annually
Landing Zone Operations	Annual
EVOC	Tri-Annual
Culminating Training Events	
Structural Live Fire	Semi-Annual
Hazardous Materials	Semi-Annual
Technical Rescue	Semi-Annual
Provide Instructional/Subject Matter Expert Assistance to Operations	
Firefighting Operations	As Needed

CAPTAINS

All METLs assigned to Firefighters as well as the METLs listed below

METL	FREQUENCY
Fire Officer Development	
Command and Control/Leadership Training	Quarterly
Incident Safety Officer Training	Annual
Supervisor Development	Tri-Annual

Chief Officers

METL	FREQUENCY
Fire Officer Development	
Command and Control/Leadership Training	Quarterly
Incident Safety Officer Training	Annually
Supervisor Development	Tri-Annual
Emergency Medical Technician	
Emergency Medical Technician	Monthly
CPR	Bi-Annual
Operational Requirements	
Structural Firefighting	Quarterly
Pre-Incident Planning	Quarterly
Fire Inspection Procedures	Annually
Specific Hazardous Processes/Permits	Annually
Breathing Apparatus	Annually
Fire Department Communications	Annually
EVOC	Tri-Annual
Culminating Training Events	
Structural Live Fire	Semi-Annual
Hazardous Materials	Semi-Annual
Confined Space	Annually
Provide Instructional/Subject Matter Expert Assistance to Operations	
Incident Command/Leadership	Semi-Annual
Firefighting Operations	Semi-Annual

Appendix A: Suggested Training Requirements

FIRE INSPECTORS & A/C of FIRE PREVENTION

METL	FREQUENCY
Fire Prevention	
Fire Inspections	Annually
Public Education	Annually
Engineer Plans Review	Annually
Fire Investigations	Annually
Fire Officer Development	
Command and Control/Leadership Training	Quarterly
Incident Safety Officer Training	Annually
Emergency Medical Technician	
Emergency Medical Technician	Monthly
CPR	Bi-Annual
Operational Requirements	
Structural Firefighting	Semi-Annual
Breathing Apparatus	Annually
Fire Department Communications	Annually
Hazardous Materials	Annually
Confined Space	Annually
Wildland Firefighting	Annually
Vehicle/Industrial Rescue	Annually
EVOC	Tri-Annual
Landing Zone Operations	Annually
Fire Apparatus Driver Operator	Quarterly
Culminating Training Events	
Structural Live Fire	Annually
Hazardous Materials	Annually
Confined Space	Annually
Provide Instructional/Subject Matter Expert Assistance	
Fire Inspection Procedures	Annually
Building Construction	Annually
Pre-Incident Planning	As Needed
Specific Hazardous Processes/Permits	As Needed
Operational Training Assistance	As Needed

About the Author

Dave McGlynn was born in Rahway, NJ and grew up in the Iselin section of Woodbridge Township, NJ. He is the youngest of four, with two older brothers Rich and Pete and an older sister Kelly. His parents are Richard (Rick) McGlynn who was born and raised in Hastings, PA and served in the US Army during Vietnam and his mother Pamela (Pam) McGlynn who was born and raised in the Greenville section of Jersey City, NJ. Dave was raised by two "baby-boomers" so hard work and dedication were values bestowed upon him and his siblings. As a student Dave struggled greatly, he was written off by many teachers and peers. This is what gave him his passion to want to develop others. Dave's mission is to offer the opportunity to those in his path to grow and become the best version of themselves. Literally relating to those who were considered "undesirables" is an advantage of Dave's, as he uses this level of empathy as a tool to help motivate others both in his lectures, teachings, articles, but in life. Dave believes in true mentorship, he has been the recipient of a few different mentors throughout his life, and attributes a lot of his successes and opportunities to their constant guidance. In addition to his parents and his wife, he dedicates a lot of what he does to the positive educational role models he had like Mr. Wade IlVento, Mrs. Ann Dinicola, and Frank Ricci.

Dave has been in fire and emergency services since 2001. He has served in both municipal and federal fire departments. Having had experiences while working under some of the best and worst training officers and leaders out there. His passion for training and leading firefighters has helped inspire others throughout the fire service.

Dave is the owner of Passion in Leading, LLC which is a motivational professional development company that offers instruction on leadership, networking, and training program development. He writes on leadership and training program development and has spoken on both topics throughout the United States.

He has two children, Angela and Michael and is married to his Brooklyn-born Puerto Rican wife, Krissy. Everything he does in his life is dedicated to them first.

Bibliography

Center for Public Safety Excellence. (2020, November). *Commission on Fire Accreditation International 10th Edition Model.* Retrieved from Center for Public Safety Excellence: https://www.cpse.org/accreditation/cfai10/

Chung, K. (2015, March 14). *Marketing Your Art the Right Way.* Retrieved from Quote by General George Patton: http://marketingtrw.com/blog/i-dont-measure-a-mans-success-by-how-high-he-climbs-but-how-high-he-bounces-when-he-hits-bottom-george-s-patton/

Damani, A. (2023). *Author Name: Galileo Galilei.* Retrieved from Anand Damani: https://www.ananddamani.com/quotes/galileo-galilei-you-cannot-teach-a-man-anything/

Franklin, Benjamin; The Secret Libraries. (2016). *Benjamin Franklin quotes... Vol.23: Motivational and inspirational life quotes by Benjamin Franklin.* CreateSpace Independent Publishing Platform. Retrieved from https://books.google.com/books/about/Benjamin_Franklin_Quotes_Vol_23.html?id=EAIZMQAACAAJ

Gariano, F. (2021, September 11). *Former White House chief of staff recalls Bush's bullhorn speech at ground zero.* Retrieved from Today all day: https://www.today.com/news/former-white-house-chief-staff-bush-s-bullhorn-speech-9-t230732

Graham, G. (2020). *High-risk, low-frequency events in public safety.* Retrieved from Lexipol: https://www.lexipol.com/resources/blog/high-risk-low-frequency-events-in-public-safety/

Jordan, M. (1994). *Michael Jordan.* Retrieved from AZ Quotes: https://www.azquotes.com/quote/150627

Lasky, R. (2006). *Pride and ownership: A firefighter's love of the job.* Rochelle Park, NJ: Fire Engineering Books.

Letterkenny Fire IAFF Local F-170. (2020-2023). *Letterkenny Fire IAFF Local F-170.* Retrieved from Facebook: https://www.facebook.com/IaffLocalF170

OS Web Designing. (2016, October 28). *Once You Stop Leaning, You Start Dying.* Retrieved from Medium: https://medium.com/@OSWebDesigner/once-you-stop-learning-you-start-dying-617f0dbdf2a6

Parseghian, A. (2023). *Top 2 Ara Parseghian Quotes (2024 Update).* Retrieved from quotefancy: https://quotefancy.com/ara-parseghian-quotes

Sinek, S. (2009, September). *How great leaders inspire action.* (S. Sinek, Performer) TEDx Puget Sound, Puget Sound, WA, USA. Retrieved from https://www.ted.com/talks/simon_sinek_how_great_leaders_inspire_action

West Point Professional Firefighters. (2016-2020). *West Point Professional Firefighters.* Retrieved from Facebook: https://www.facebook.com/westpointbravest

Wilson, W. (1914, March 20). Speech to the National Press Club. *The Independent, 77.*

www.ingramcontent.com/pod-product-compliance
Lightning Source LLC
Chambersburg PA
CBHW040903020526
44114CB00037B/39